REMEMBERING
LYNDON

REMEMBERING
LYNDON
A GLANCE BACK IN TIME

Harriet Fletcher Fisher

Published by The History Press
Charleston, SC 29403
www.historypress.net

Copyright © 2008 by Harriet Fletcher Fisher
All rights reserved

Cover design by Natasha Momberger.

Images courtesy of the author unless otherwise stated.

First published 2008

Manufactured in the United Kingdom

ISBN 978.1.59629.512.4

Library of Congress Cataloging-in-Publication Data

Fisher, Harriet F.
Remembering Lyndon : a glance back in time / Harriet Fletcher Fisher.
p. cm.
ISBN 978-1-59629-512-4
1. Lyndon (Vt.)--History--Anecdotes. 2. Lyndon (Vt.)--Social life and customs--Anecdotes. 3. Lyndon (Vt.)--Biography--Anecdotes. I. Title.
F59.L96F57 2008
974.3'34--dc22
 2008021147

Notice: The information in this book is true and complete to the best of our knowledge. It is offered without guarantee on the part of the author or The History Press. The author and The History Press disclaim all liability in connection with the use of this book.

All rights reserved. No part of this book may be reproduced or transmitted in any form whatsoever without prior written permission from the publisher except in the case of brief quotations embodied in critical articles and reviews.

CONTENTS

Introduction 7

Positive Look at Lyndonville 9
What to See in Our Classy Town 11
Lyndonville Grew Around a Tall Chimney 17
A Walk on Depot Street, circa 1895 25
When the Lights Came On in Lyndonville in 1896 29
The Old Camp Meetings, Railroad Grove and Powers Park 37
W. Irving Powers Envisioned a Park For All 43
The Old Log House 47
The Village Poet 51
The Community Building—Corner Garage 55
Entertainment Was Just Around the Corner 61
Dancing the New Year In 65
The Village Hall Was a Cultural Center 67
The Masonic Building 73
The Journey of the Covered Bridge 77
The Greening of the Gem 81
Christmas in Lyndonville 85
The Snowflake 91
Family Doctor of an Earlier Day 95
Dr. Venila Lovina Shores's Legacy 101
The Late Victorian "Working Man's House" 105
The Vermont Hooked Rug Industry 107
The Victory Corps Ski Team 111

Contents

The Old Meetinghouse of 1809	115
The Sleeping Babe Monument, Emblem of Eternal Rest	119
Camp Vail and Soldiers of the Soil	123
The News in Lyndon	129
The Oldest Church in Town	133
The Academies in Lyndon	139
There Was a Tavern in the Town	145
Lyndon Maple Candies	149
Ye Olde Bricke Tea Shoppe	155

INTRODUCTION

My interest in local history began in my childhood, when I would hear my father and my aunt reminiscing about their days growing up on the farm. My aunt, fifteen years older than my father, could tell him many things that he didn't remember, especially about some older family members, so I sort of got to know them, too. When I grew up, I found I liked researching in many sources for information, talking to "old-timers" and studying old photos and old postcards for clues. I did this not to live in the past, but to know what it was like. Going to the creamery with my dad was part of it, too; as we drove through Lyndonville, he would talk about what it was like when he was growing up. I got to know a lot of older people. We'd stop by a store and I would hear them talking about town affairs, or about a new store or business in town. When I was "down street" with my mother, she often stopped to talk with people we met along the way.

This book comprises many articles I have written about past events or people in Lyndon. They have appeared in different publications, such as the *Caledonian-Record*, the *Lyndon Independent*, the *Northland Journal*, the *Lyndon Legacy* and others.

POSITIVE LOOK AT LYNDONVILLE

The card on the following page, postmarked July 27, 1914, represented a positive look at Lyndonville. "I want you to come to Lyndonville, the classy town," it says.

That would be a good card to send to friends and relatives. We could write on the back, "I want you to come to Lyndonville to see how the village has taken a positive stance in 2000—new sidewalks, streets newly repaved, flowering trees along Depot Street, attractive green-and-white banners saying, 'Welcome to Lyndonville.'"

We could further add, "While you are here, be sure to note the beautiful Bandstand Park, and the newly landscaped lawn at the municipal building, thanks to generous donations by Lyndon Woman's Club and the Lyndonville Rotary Club, and thanks to Elliott's landscaping expertise. Notice the little park at the intersection of South and Broad Streets, newly landscaped and named Norrie Park in memory of longtime village water superintendent Bill Norrie."

We are indeed a "classy" town.

Come to the classy town.

WHAT TO SEE IN OUR CLASSY TOWN

When coming into an unfamiliar town, a visitor might wonder, "What does this place have that would pique my curiosity?"

Would visitors like to see in Lyndonville exact replicas in bronze of what is known as the most beautiful animal statue in the world? There are two replicas of *Lion of the Republic*, the original statue being held in Florence, Italy, and originally sculpted by the Renaissance artist Donatello. Our lions stand by the Lyndonville Bank (Community Bank) on Broad Street. They arrived in Lyndonville from Florence in 1905, and were placed at the beautiful bank, then Lyndonville National Bank (newly built in 1895 after a disastrous fire). The lions came courtesy of the cashier Luther B. Harris, the casting having been overseen in Italy by the famous sculptor Larkin Mead.

Across the street, one might stop at the veterans' memorial, which was dedicated to all Lyndon-area men and women who served in the armed forces. The memorial was designed by Paul Aubin, who drafted many other architectural features in our town.

Work of Lyndon's nationally renowned, award-winning artist, Beth Robbins, is seen in the Cobleigh Public Library—not one but three stained-glass windows depicting people of various ages enjoying books and companionship. While in the library, a visitor may note the handsome details of the building itself, as well as paintings and artifacts that were given by Lyndon's famous resident, Theodore N. Vail, the founder of American Telephone & Telegraph Company. The building of the library, dedicated in 1906, was funded by Eber W. Cobleigh and named for him. It took the place of Silsby's Livery Stable—quite a different use of that corner on Depot and Main Streets.

The Mathewson Block, facing Depot Street, is dated 1869, and two other three-story brick buildings form the Norris Block, built after the 1894 fire; the

Remembering Lyndon

Above: "These two lions stand in front of the bank and were brought from Florence, Italy by my father when he was there just a year ago today. Yours, Bill, 9/20/05." Written by William S. Harris, son of Luther B. Harris.

Left: The Veterans' Memorial in Memorial Park in Lyndonville (formerly Railroad Park). *Courtesy of the* Lyndon Independent.

A Glance Back in Time

The dedication of the Veterans' Memorial. *From left:* selectman Bruce James; Woman's Club President Virginia Jarrosak; Pete and Marilyn Kelly, representing the American Legion; Lyndon historian Ruth Hopkins McCarty; Craig Langtine, from Passumpsic Bank; and designer of the memorial, Paul Aubin, 1991.

Dodge & Watson (Gebbie) Block sports the year 1897. Those bricks laid in a curved pattern still seen next to the sidewalk on the Elm Street side of the 1897 block were once placed over basement windows below the sidewalk. There were iron railings around those places so people wouldn't accidently step into those deep recesses made for light to enter the windows into the basement.

On Main Street is what today we call Bandstand Park, where, if you are here between mid-June and mid-August, you may enjoy an outdoor band concert on Wednesday evenings at 7:00 p.m. Though many tall, stately elm trees once graced the park, they are now gone due to the Dutch elm disease. The Lyndon Woman's Club and others have planted trees, shrubs and flowers to keep the park beautiful. Kids like to splash around in the fountain pool. Why not, on a warm summer evening?

You might stop in Lyndon Center to admire another bronze statue, a replica of Pietro Tacca's famous wild boar fountain (*Il Porcellino*) in Florence, Italy, again courtesy of Luther B. Harris. Born in Sutton, Harris was a Civil War soldier and a prisoner of the Confederacy who survived and became a railroad postal clerk for the Union Pacific Railroad. Lyndon became his home. He was a connoisseur of art and an art collector. He liked to see his town enhanced by these beautiful works of art—the lions and wild boar statue. He developed a little park specifically for the boar fountain.

Remembering Lyndon

The wild boar fountain. *From left:* Carolyn Frey; club president, Colleen Murphy; Andrea Lotti; Lyndon Historical Society president, Virginia Campbell Downs; heading the Seed and Weed Boar Historic Garden Project, Phyllis Josselyn; from the Lyndon selectboard, Martha Feltus.

The park made an impression on Theodore Roosevelt. On August 12, 1912, after speaking in Barton during the Bull Moose campaign, he was scheduled to stop at depot square in Lyndonville, where people waited for the two- or three-minute stop he intended to make there. The Roosevelt party missed the road to Lyndonville, came through Lyndon Center and stopped where the road divided. Roosevelt was so impressed with the little park and the Florentine boar fountain that during his address to thousands of people in St. Johnsbury, he spent some time in praise of the park and fountain. Newspapers reported that the fifteen-minute delay in reaching St. Johnsbury was due to the inspection of the park and fountain.

Today the park flowers and shrubs are well tended by the Seed and Weed Garden Club. The club made it a historic garden project and won an award for its work.

Turning the corner at Lyndon Center, look up at the classical style of the main building of Lyndon Institute, an independent secondary school chartered in 1867 with several campuses and thirty-four buildings. All of the buildings are in use and some are being restored to their original external appearance while the interiors are being adapted to best application for other school uses.

There at Lyndon Center stands the oldest public building in town, with the designation over the door reading, "Town House, 1809." It was built as a meetinghouse for four religious denominations (the town put in some money so it could be used for town meetings as well). It is now used for other public meetings, particularly by the Lyndon Historical Society. It is also used by Lyndon Institute, especially for the cultural arts dance classes.

On the lawn in front of the Town House is the 1991 Lyndon Bicentennial Memorial executed by sculptor Ramon Geremia. It depicts many phases of Lyndon's development through the years—education, the railroad, the Morgan horse, maple sugaring, Lyndonville's famous Bag Balm and more.

Behind the Town House is the cemetery, the only one in Lyndon except for the Catholic cemetery in another part of town. Here at Lyndon Center Cemetery are some handsome stones and memorials, including one much-noted monument, *The Sleeping Babe*, executed by stonecutter Gratis P. Spencer. The babe reposes on the top. Around the perimeter, Spencer inscribed atheist ideas that so offended some people that they tried to obliterate them. Although they did not succeed completely, some words have been worn off by the elements. However, the words are preserved by some historians who kept them on record.

Near the Town House is the old horse shed, the hearse house and the schoolhouse of 1858. The horse shed and hearse house are newly renovated with modern cemetery equipment, and the District Six Schoolhouse is restored so visitors may be treated to the "one-room school experience."

Nearby is a late-Victorian "working man's home," left to the town by the builder's daughter, Venila L. Shores, PhD. She was a history professor at Florida State University who worked on Lyndon town history while she was at home during the summer and also after her retirement. She left the house to the town for the purposes of creating a museum.

We haven't forgotten the five covered bridges still left in the town of Lyndon, often sought out by covered-bridge enthusiasts for photos. Two were saved when new sections of road were built to bypass the bridges, one was moved to another location and two are still on the town highway system.

LYNDONVILLE GREW AROUND A TALL CHIMNEY

Something new was happening in a hayfield north of Lyndon Corner. Charles M. Chase—diligent newspaperman that he was, and editor and publisher of the *Vermont Union*—was paying close attention. The paper, published every Friday, reported on September 7, 1866, "The tall chimney is beginning to rise above the pile of bricks around the railroad shop." On October 19, he wrote, "The long chimney at the railroad shops is completed—92 feet high—and much the tallest pile of bricks in this county." The chimney stood high above the growing business that the Connecticut & Passumpsic Rivers Railroad (C&PRR) was building in the town of Lyndon.

When fire destroyed the C&PRR shops at St. Johnsbury in March 1866, the company looked for a new place to rebuild that could accommodate the expansion of its railroad operations. A suitable situation was found in Lyndon: more than 334 acres of farmland, owned by Benjamin Sanborn. What was a misfortune in St. Johnsbury became the beginning of a new village in the township of Lyndon.

The heart of this village that became Lyndonville started beating at 3:57 p.m. on Wednesday, August 1, 1866. The corner brick—the first brick—was laid on the foundation for the railroad shops. The new village started to grow in all directions from the tall chimney, or as far as the 334 acres went, and every week Editor Chase reported on the progress. He wrote about new machines being brought into the shops, what new streets were laid out and who was building houses and where.

Chase continued to keep tabs on the progress. He probably drove his horse to the construction site by whatever farm road led there. By December, a new road was laid out from the Corner, crossing the Passumpsic River near the Lyndon station, and people could head directly north to the

The tall chimney, ninety-two feet high—the start of a new village.

"new village." The company opened East Street and erected six cottages for workers. Until there were houses for all the workers, the railroad ran a commuter train every day from St. Johnsbury. Chase may even have rode on this train from the Lyndon station to talk to workers and view the progress of construction, returning to the Corner by a later train.

By fall, George B. Walker's hotel was up. It "promises to make a grand show on the flat when it is covered." Mr. Sanborn had dug the cellar for his "dwelling house" on a lot reserved for him during the sale to the railroad.

In January 1867, the roundhouse was completed, machinery was being set up and a reservoir was ready for water. "It will soon be let in and the Passumpsic road can boast of the best water works in Vermont," Chase wrote. "About the first of March the workmen can begin the work of railroad repairs in the new shops." (I remember two big reservoirs, one in our pasture just up the hill from East Street, and the other just off High Street.)

Planning an attractive village, the railroad company planted trees on both sides of the streets. "They go to work systematically to make a beautiful and convenient village," Chase commented on May 24. The next week he wrote, "A new bridge north of the shops is nearly ready for travel." When finished it would complete a new road from Lyndon Corner to the new village, along to the three-way junction with its choices of heading for West Burke, East Burke or for circling back to Lyndon Centre (later "Center" in the modern spelling).

The Reverend Perrin B. Fisk and his wife Harriet, driving from Peacham and coming through Lyndon Centre on their way to a conference in East Burke in June 1867, could see "bustling activity" on the other side of the river. Two days later, when returning, they found the bridge completed enough to drive the horse and buggy across it and view the activity firsthand.

Reverend Fisk wrote later about seeing ox teams plowing and scraping Main Street from the bridge to a point opposite the roundhouse. They saw lots on Main Street, mostly vacant or with piles of lumber accumulating on them, or with cellars partly completed.

"I wonder what denomination will be enterprising enough to take up work in this village soon," Reverend Fisk said to his wife. "Why don't you do it?" she asked. Just for fun, they selected a site for a church and a parsonage as if they were really going to settle here. Coincidently, when the church was actually built five years later it was located very close to where they had chosen. And Reverend Fisk was the first minister of this new Lyndonville Congregational Church.

In July, the boiler shop (80 by 32 feet) was completed and ready for the brick masons. The paint shop was 40 by 56 feet. The lumber sheds, each 125 by 40 feet, were raised and a car house was being framed. "We do not recollect the length," Chase said," but it is tremendously long." L.P. Brown put up a wholesale store near the depot. Benjamin Sanborn erected a fine edifice on the lot reserved for him.

Since its beginning, the new village had no name. Some thought of Keyes Ville or Keyesville, in honor of Henry Keyes, president of the railroad. It was also thought that this village ought to have its own post office. On January 10, 1868, George B. Walker signed an application for a post office. The document said, "The proposed office will be called Lyndonville." The U.S. Post Office Department announced his appointment as postmaster on April 13, and he set up the office in his hotel.

By that time, the passenger depot was nearly finished at a cost of $20,000, and "is far the best on the road and probably the best in the state." A large furnace heated the whole building with steam pipes and hot air registers. There were rooms for officers of several branches of the railroad business; four rooms were supplied with large fireproof vaults. On April 10, 1868, Chase wrote that the freight station was completed, a dozen houses were built and all lots were sold on the east side of Main Street, from the common (today's Bandstand Park) to the grove. The railroad grove, the scene of many gatherings, is now Powers Park.

In April 1868, Chase reported that three fine houses were to be immediately built by Horace Alden, master mechanic; H. Hastings, cashier; and A.H. Perry, superintendent. Two of them were to be brick. These are the three houses on the north side opposite Bandstand Park. Chase wrote,

> *C.A. Page and C.H. Green have raised houses on East Street, the Railroad band gives concerts in Walker's Hotel. W.H. Clough offers for sale a nice little cottage near the depot. Good chance for some mechanic who wants to*

The railroad created a village. This is Church Street, circa 1900. The Congregational Church, facing, left of center; back of Methodist Church, right of center.

A Glance Back in Time

> *reside near the railroad shops. Royal Ayer, D.N. Trull, James Randall, Wright and Cilley and others have put up residences this season.*

Walker put the finishing touches on the main part of his hotel. "It is brick, 60´ square, three stories high with modern conveniences—each story provided with earth closets and water runs into all the large rooms. There are 60 large and airy sleeping rooms, furnished with carpets, mattresses and furniture, the whole house warmed by a furnace."

Editor Chase continued to report in 1869 about those who were building houses or businesses and the names have a familiar ring today, either from history or descendants in the area:

> *G.L. Mathewson begins drawing the brick for his block, Dr. Trull's house is well along, Ayer's house is so far finished that he is now occupying it, John Sleeper has built a barn on the lot just north of Chesley on Main Street. In the spring he will erect a dwelling there. W. H. Fletcher rents the north store in Mathewson's Block and is ready to put in a stock of goods as soon as the building is ready.*
>
> *The building in the village has been so rapid that no opportunity has yet been found to fence them in. When the fence building begins and the dooryards laid out and cared for, the general appearance will be greatly improved.*

It was generally the custom in those days to fence in the dooryards for appearance. Fences also discouraged horses from pulling over from the street for a snack of grass on someone's lawn.

The village continued to grow. George Weeks built a store on Broadway (now Broad Street). He later sold it to Aaron Twombly, who then sold it to Salmon Stern. Walker started a velocipede school in his hotel; at a velocipede race, George Hastings won a silver cup. A Calico Ball was announced to be held in Walker's Hotel. The Lyndonville Band, first referred to as the Railroad Band, began a series of concerts on Thursdays. Religious denominations began building their churches in this new location. A wooden schoolhouse with two large rooms on the first floor was built very close to the site of the brick graded school that replaced it in 1905, now the municipal offices.

The railroad company wanted and planned for an attractive village, not a "shacktown" created by rapid growth. This can be borne out by an example in the deed of my great-uncle William H. Fletcher for a corner lot he bought from the C&PRR Company on October 28, 1869. The deed stated that he was not to build a house nearer than twenty feet to either street or less than two stories in front, otherwise the deed would be null and void. Uncle William built a two-story ell first, and then added a three-story front! He sold the house to Harley E. Folsom and Jennie (Darling) Folsom in 1887. Mr. Folsom had become superintendent of the Passumpsic division of the railroad in 1872, at age twenty-two, after serving as clerk in the freight office for two years. The Folsoms moved the Fletcher house and built a new Dutch-style abode.

"This little village which is springing into importance is beginning to take form and beauty, the main street is already filled with buildings," said Charles M. Chase in 1868.

In 1869, he said, "This little village, in two years, has grown from a hayfield into a prosperous little village."

We are fortunate to have the historic details of the building of Lyndonville, reported by newspaper editor Charles M. Chase.

A WALK ON DEPOT STREET, CIRCA 1895

The photo on the following page appeared in *Images of Lyndon*, but perhaps some people have an interest in learning even more information. Later photos show the street neat and trim with new buildings. In 1924, though, half of this street would burn down again and a third major look for Depot Street would follow.

It looks like a quiet day on Depot Street in 1895, months after the fire in November of 1894. No one appears to be working today, and we see only a horse, a delivery wagon and some men looking things over. Let's say it is Sunday afternoon—a good time to walk along Depot Street and look at the progress of reconstruction. I think we will be able to see into the future of this street.

We'll start at the corner of Depot and Main Streets (the lower left corner in the photo). Here is the Old Corner Boarding House. It did not burn—maybe the flames had their fill by the time they reached this far end of the street. It is H.L. Parker's building whose store ads we find in old newspapers. A sign says "Harness Shop."

One day a canopy will be added along the front of Wilson's Harness and Shoe Repair Shop; the entrance will be on the street level under the canopy. Homer will also be a longtime director of the Lyndonville Military Band. A stairway leads upstairs to the boardinghouse. This building will be torn down in the late 1940s and the Plaza Theater built in its place. The theater building will later become White's Market.

The next building is a temporary one for someone's business, but we see it remodeled in the future, perhaps several times. It will become Paul Aubin's Jewelry Store, later David Pezdirtz's and then Kennedy's Jewelry; a hundred years from now it will be Lyndonville Video.

Next is Tarbell's Block, three stories high. Here G.B. Allyn will have a "Furniture & Caskets, Pianos, Wallpaper and Undertaking" business.

Lyndonville recovering after the sweeping fire of 1894.

Hosford's photography studio will be located upstairs. The future shows that a fire damages the top section that will change the building into a two-story block. In about one hundred years or so, Jolly's Books, the Rag Bag, Vermont Screen Prints and Debbie's Beauty Boutique will do business here, with even more changes later.

Now we come to the two-story block under construction. Years from now, there will be a double store here, with Moore and Tripp men's apparel in one part and ladies' wear in the other. Customers will move from one to the other, either from the inside or from the street. This block will contain Russell's Men's Shop and Russell's Drug Store, the latter unfortunately to be destroyed by fire in 1968. A new block will be built by the Bona family.

We are now here by the two brick buildings: one is the Cheney Bros. Block that houses their drugstore. At some time McCann's grocery store will do business in the west end and the Gold Medal Flour sign will be painted high on the side of the building, still visible by 1998. Cheney Bros. Drug Store will be owned in turn by A.W. Edmunds, Dennis Stevens and finally, Horace "Bud" Fichera. Looking ahead, we can see Fabrictown doing business in both parts of this space. The block will be owned and renovated by Vincent Matteis.

The brick building sitting tightly beside it is the Weeks Block. When the block is finished, the first-floor corner section next to Church Street will be the Lyndonville Post Office until 1960, when the new post office will be built on Broad Street. The Weeks Block will only be two stories high for a time, but a third story will be added, bringing it to a height even with its closest neighbor. At a future date, John Norris will own this block for many years.

A Glance Back in Time

Now we cross Church Street and come to the beginning construction of the brick Masonic Block that promises to be a handsome addition to the village, and fly the American flag on the tall pole. The Ide Block, next in line, is almost finished. From this point, we can't see the passenger station that is beyond the Ide Block. A tall tree stands on the small park lawn in front of Ide's.

Across the track is the Union House Hotel, which will be known as Pleasant View House and by other names, depending on the owners. We see it as Gracie's Inn when it burns down in 1969.

Looking up above Depot Street, the large tenement house that we can see on the hill will burn someday. The St. Elisabeth Catholic Church, built in 1892, stands tall above the village. St. Martin's School beside the church is now closed, but it will soon be moved across the street and made into a residence. The three houses seen on East Street in front of St. Elisabeth's, will be taken down to make a church parking lot.

As we start back down Depot Street, on the other side, there is one house on the corner of East and Depot Streets and one on the corner of Williams Street. Now we cross the railroad track and come to Depot Park. It will have a future as Memorial Park. The temporary building here is for bank business, and it was set up after the fire. (The tree beside it easily reminds you of the photo that appears in *Images of Lyndon*). Now we cross Broad Street and come to the corner of Broad and Depot Streets. I understand that Salmon Stern will build a fine three-story block here soon.

The Eaton Block, next in line, is three stories high; beside it, with the double porches, is Webb's Hotel, the first building to be completed after the fire. The fire started in Webb's Hotel, but the replacement looks very much like the one that burned.

Now we cross Elm Street and find the first temporary building that was ready for business after the fire. This is where H.B. Hutchins, who had a store in the burned Hoyt Block, continued selling groceries until he could relocate. Dodge & Watson has bought the burned-out Hoyt Block lot and will build a three-story brick block for his furniture store, now doing business in the Mathewson Block. The date 1897, raised in gilded wood, will appear high on the structure of the Dodge & Watson Block. Many years from now it will be Emmons and Hebert Plumbing and Heating. In time it will become the Gebbie Block.

Finally, we come to David Silsby's Livery Stable on the corner, in the lower right part of the photo. In 1905, Silsby will sell the stable and lot to the town. He will agree to take down the stable and clear the lot because the library benefactor, Eber Cobleigh, will request that the library be ready for use by 1906.

We can easily see from this walk in 1895 that Depot Street will be humming again when all of this construction is finished. You might say it will become the "second Depot Street," with a completely different appearance from the street originally begun in 1866.

WHEN THE LIGHTS CAME ON IN LYNDONVILLE IN 1896

"The village streets, stores, and residences will ere long be illuminated with electricity by turning a button. Goodbye kerosene, lamp burners, broken chimneys, litter, dirt and danger"—so said the *Vermont Union* on November 1, 1895. "Electric lights were turned on for the first time Tuesday evening [February 25, 1896], and worked finely with the exception of a few residences where the connections were not perfect," was the report in the paper for February 28. "The lights run true and steady, without the ups and downs so often observed in other plants."

Electric lights were not completely new to Lyndonville. A big 1883 Fourth of July celebration advertised in the *Union*: "Grand exhibition of Electric Light by the American Electric Light Company. It makes night equal to midday and the effect is wonderful. Everybody in northern Vermont who had never seen electric lights should come."

After a day of lively events on that Fourth of July, about one thousand people gathered that evening in the cleaned and decorated railroad paint shop to hear a concert by a thirty-piece band from Montreal. The shop was "AS LIGHT AS DAY," provided by four electric lights suspended overhead in the paint shop; eight lights between there and the depot gave people a well-lighted approach to the concert. "To those who had never seen the power of the electric light, the exhibition alone was worth the price of the day's entertainment," said the *Union*.

In 1889, the railroad company in Lyndonville sent a man from St. Johnsbury—it had started its light company in 1888—to arrange for the installation of electric lights. These 104 lights were turned on in October of 1889 and distributed in the paint shop, boiler shop, blacksmith shop, tin shop, tool room, wood shop, pattern room, engine room, machine shop and the office; they were presumably powered by some by kind of battery system. How much easier it must have been to work during the dark hours.

In the spring of 1895, the village of Lyndonville began taking electric lights very seriously. At first, a committee talked about steam power, but soon realized that this would be too expensive. The committee then talked to C.T. Wilder about his pulp mill and the water privilege at the Great Falls, which had a drop of sixty-two feet in less than thirty rods.

Finally, in the fall, a committee—including S. Stern, M.L. Stearns and L.C. Todd—was authorized to accept an offer made by C.T. Wilder to lease (with an option to buy) his company's mill and the water privilege of the Great Falls. While waiting for authority from the legislature for the village to borrow the necessary funds, Stearns, Stern, Todd and J.T. Gleason formed a company and gave their personal note for $18,000. They held the note until the village could take over.

With these arrangements made, a crew of about eight men began clearing the mill, tearing out the mill wheels and installing, at a cost of $2,500, a set of Rodney Hunt Manufacturing Company's twenty-four-inch twin wheels, warranted to develop 640 horsepower. They repaired the building, finished off a dynamo room and put in a Westinghouse lighting arc machine and two Stanley machines, each two thousand incandescent "lighters," as they called them.

In the meantime, another crew was setting poles running from the mill to Lyndonville village, crisscrossing the railroad tracks and the Passumpsic

The first dynamo was installed in the former Wilder Mill in 1896.

A Glance Back in Time

The first streetlights were carbon arc lamps.

River a couple of times in the process. As the poles were set they began stringing the wires.

"It is expected that within 8 weeks the village will be equipped with a modern lighting apparatus and then the street lamps can be used on moonlight nights without comment," said the *Union*, but the plant was not ready in early January as first planned. It was in February when the wheels were set and the water was let in, but there was still a delay in waiting for shafting and belts. "Inside of a week," said the *Union* on February 7, 1896, "they will begin to generate electricity and all can get ready to hurrah for the new lights."

In April of 1896, the village assumed ownership and elected as commissioners M.L. Stearns, J.T. Gleason and S.B. Hutchins, putting them in charge of the entire system. The 640 horsepower was more than was necessary for running the thirty-four arc streetlights in the village and the incandescent lights in residences and stores, leaving about 500 horsepower left over to rent out. The Lyndonville Board of Trade began corresponding with some people, hoping to start some manufactories here, and began soliciting people in outlying districts to wire their homes and businesses.

A set of rates interesting to us today was set and published in the *Union* at the time:

> *Stores and offices: each light, $3.00; a cellar or back room: $2.00; hotels: a first light in each room except sleeping rooms, $3.00, and extras thereafter, $2.00; first light in each sleeping room, $2.00; extras thereafter, $1.00; each light in bathroom or water closet, $3.00; extras, $2.00; barn or stable: $3.00; public halls: each light $1.00; private homes: first light in each living room or hall, $3.00; extras, $1.50; each light in barn, shed or cellar, $1.00, first light in sleeping, back room or pantry, $1.50; extras, $1.00.*

Residences, stores and other places outside the village of Lyndonville were metered. For example, where I grew up, the Fletcher Farm, had been wired in the 1890s (the first farm in the town of Lyndon to use electricity). The meter was on a wall in the attic on the third floor.

Meter rates were two-thirds of a cent per hour per light, with a minimum rate of thirty-five dollars per year for stores and fourteen dollars per year for all others. Meters of ordinary size cost about fourteen dollars, to be furnished by the owner of the house or by the village at rental of 10 percent of cost with privilege of buying.

Kerosene streetlamps had been used where business owners wanted some light, probably furnished by themselves. The lamps held very little fuel, and it is thought today that they were lighted when needed and put out when the business closed. As a teenager, W. Edward Riley lighted the one by the bank. This lamp was given to the Lyndon Historical Society by Mr. Riley's daughter, Patricia Riley Leslie, and can be seen at the Shores Memorial Museum.

In the annual town report for the year ending December 31, 1899, the electric commissioners J.W. Copeland, John Cleary and C.G. Norris said, "It has been the endeavor of your commissioners to manage the business affairs of the electric plant, during the year 1899, as nearly as possible as they would if they owned the property. We know of no safer rule to follow. It is to be regretted that so few real estate owners patronize the electric plant. Out of 54 dwellings on Main street only eleven use the electric lights. The plant is village property, and pride in its success ought to cause it to receive a hearty support."

The commissioners strongly advised that the village pay for their arc lights and for lighting Music Hall with the same rates that others pay. "You have paid them $600 for lighting, a ridiculous price. It has been your custom to have your lights for a mere pittance and borrow to meet the deficiency. Without doubt from $1500 to $2000 of your present debt is for street

A Glance Back in Time

The new station was first built in 1915.

lighting." The commissioners pulled no punches when they added, "No business man would conduct his business that way, if he did he would soon be in the poor house. There seems to be a strong disposition to consider the electric plant a free horse and ride it to death."

In that same report, the commissioners noted that the station was recently visited by an agent of one of the large electric companies; he gave as his opinion that it was the best-equipped station in Vermont.

Also noted was a contract that was made with the Boston & Maine Railroad to furnish power for running the machinery of the shops and lighting the shops at the rate of $2,000 per year for five years. Apparently the railroad gave up the do-it-yourself system installed in 1889.

The *Vermont Union-Journal* of May 26, 1915, gives a full account of the construction of the new municipal electric plant, and what it contained, at the Great Falls. In charge were commissioners H.J. Hubbard, H.E. Graves and H.W. Lyster. The report also said that it is hard to estimate just how much past and present prosperity of the village of Lyndonville is due to its municipal electric and water plants.

"A large share of the credit for building up the present prosperous, up-to-date modern village, from the ruins of the old one destroyed by fire [in 1894] must go to the enterprise its citizens have shown in installing these properties and making them succeed."

After that big fire, Lyndonville badly needed a "free horse." The electric plant earned enough to take up the bonds of the village charged against it; if no money had been diverted to other village properties, Lyndonville might have retained its charred condition much longer.

With a net income averaging $8,000 a year and its bonds and interest charge reduced to a reasonable figure, large sums were appropriated from the electric earnings for the construction of sewers, paving of streets and building of sidewalks, much of which might never have been undertaken had there been no income from this source, the *Union-Journal* explained. In later years, a sum of at least $10,000 a year was set aside for redevelopment and improvement of the electric plant when needed. In 1979, the legislature made it a law that earnings from public service plants had to be saved for improvements and redevelopment.

The 1915 *Union-Journal* described the construction of a new municipal electric plant. The difficulty in 1915 was that while the new plant was under construction, the old one in the old mill building had to keep operating. The new plant was built on a solid ledge eleven feet below water level. It was reinforced concrete and brick, and was built spanning the tailrace just south of the former plant (the mill building). Construction included a new penstock to the powerhouse.

After the big flood in November of 1927, a total of $60,000 was spent to improve the plant, and other money was allocated to rebuild the dam badly damaged in the flood.

In 1928, it was apparent that many people were "turning some buttons" for lights not listed by the light company and therefore not included in the flat-rate payments. Some may have been honest mistakes, said the commissioners, but some were meant to defraud; they began to consider metering rather than using flat rates. However, it was several years before this went into effect.

Henry E. Graves was Lyndonville Electric Plant manager from 1931 until his resignation in 1947. Leland E. Gray became manager and stayed until 1973, when Harland Titemore took over upon Gray's retirement. In 1978, present manager Ken Mason took the position. There is (as of 1998) an operator at the Great Falls Plant eight hours a day—sixteen hours in the winter—who also monitors the system load at the Vail Plant; a crew and trucks at Grove Street keep the lines in operating condition.

The Vail Plant, built by Theodore N. Vail for his own use at his property on Vail Hill, was later acquired by the Lyndonville Electric Plant. In the town report for the year 1938, commissioners D.I. Grapes, A.W. Edmunds and A.A. Cheney recommended that "each year the net earnings of the Lyndonville Electric Plant be set aside and deposited at interest in the Lyndonville Savings Bank & Trust Company to accumulate and establish a fund for the redevelopment of the then obsolete Vail Station Hydro-electric

A Glance Back in Time

Plant." That year the report showed that secondary power from the Great Falls plant was sold to Twin State Gas & Electric Co., St. Johnsbury, in the amount of $464.25.

In 1949, a new Vail plant was constructed. About 15 percent of our power was generated at Vail and Great Falls together, and the rest was purchased from other sources. Through the years, the Lyndonville Electric Plant has furnished electricity, not only for all areas within the town of Lyndon, but also for towns in the surrounding areas.

There is much more in one hundred years of operation, but I've tried to sort out some of the historical highlights and I hope everyone gets a picture of the kind of operation that our municipal electric plant required and how it all started.

THE OLD CAMP MEETINGS, RAILROAD GROVE AND POWERS PARK

Before the twenty-five acres on Main Street became Powers Park it was Railroad Grove, owned by the Connecticut & Passumpsic Rivers Railroad. Picnics, concerts and other events took place here, but the biggest events were the camp meetings. Thousands of people attended these meetings. Horses and buggies were parked all along Main Street. The railroad company owned all of what is now Lyndonville and gradually sold lots, retaining the grove until 1915. By then, C&PRR had leased to the Boston & Maine Railroad.

In the late summer of 1867, people flocked to the grove from the ten crowded cars on the train coming in the morning from the north and from the ten coming from the south. Someone counted four hundred teams, averaging three people in a wagon, between three o'clock and six o'clock, passing through Lyndon Corner and going to South Wheelock, Danville and St. Johnsbury on their return home. Newspapers said it was a "monstrous camp meeting" and reported attendance as seven thousand, possibly up to ten thousand. When the Boston & Lowell—and shortly thereafter the Boston & Maine—took over the Connecticut & Passumpsic Rivers Railroad in 1887, the same service to camp meetings was continued.

The camp meetings were a joint effort of the St. Johnsbury District Methodist Church and the railroad. The railroad company provided benches at the grove to accommodate more than three thousand campers. The entry lane at what is now Powers Park (where the tennis courts are now) was filled with hitching posts. Hitching accommodations were set on both sides of Main Street for hundreds of teams. Paul Houghton once said that he remembered when teams were hitched as far up the street to what is now the junction of Routes 5 and 114.

An association of lay people and Methodist clergy in the area organized and carried out the business of the camp meetings. For ten to fourteen

Crowds gathered at the camp meetings for religious and social assemblies.

A Glance Back in Time

days each year, the railroad rented the grove to the Methodist Association. Lyndonville was centrally located on the railroad line that ran from Wells River to Newport.

Over the years, about thirty Methodist churches in the surrounding area set up permanent cottages for their members to use during camp meetings. A building called the "temple" had an arched opening for the speakers' platform and the choir. The legend over the arch proclaimed "HOLINESS UNTO THE LORD." There was a boardwalk in front of the semicircle of buildings. Some people brought tents for shelter. The camp buildings are long gone now.

The camp was definitely meant for religious programs—services at 10:00 a.m., 2:00 p.m. and 7:00 p.m., Bible readings, prayer services and youth meetings all took place. Sermons were given by all the Methodist preachers in the area and guest ministers from as far away as St. Louis, Missouri.

Board and lodging was one dollar a day or four dollars for the duration. The Lyndonville Epworth League ran a fruit stand, grapes being the principal fruit for sale. There was no selling allowed during services and the windows were closed.

With so large a crowd, there was bound to be some trouble. One man near the grove said that his fences were repeatedly pulled down and his cows roamed the street. Newspapers reported drunks annoying the ladies, and other disorderliness. Some were arrested. However, in so large a crowd, the percentage was probably minimal for it is also reported that the police were complimented on handling the crowds.

Most people attended, it was supposed, for the spiritual uplift and the sociality. Some have said there was a lot of horse trading going on, and women swapping patterns and recipes.

In 1984, when Ruth Eastman Croft was eighty-two, she remembered that one year she was the youngest girl waiting on tables at the boardinghouse. She did not remember what was sold at the window. She remembered it was not ice cream, though, because there were no provisions for keeping ice cream under those circumstances. Someone else remembered that gingerbread was sold.

Mrs. Croft recalled how bonfires were burned at several points near the benches to keep mosquitoes away. Because the camp meetings were held late in the summer—some years even into September—"we sometimes had to hurry home to cover our gardens from the frost."

She recalled a man named Smith who went around with a hayrack to collect bedding from the church people to use for the ministers in the boardinghouse. She said the railroad guaranteed to get the farmers home in time for chores.

A Glance Back in Time

She spoke of Myrtle Aldrich of West Burke, who was blind. Aldrich played the harp and sang solos. Mrs. Croft also remembered the rows of horses with their feed bags attached.

In 1984, the Methodists celebrated the 200th year of Methodism in America with a camp meeting reenactment, with Methodist churches of the area taking part. This bicentennial camp meeting was held on September 15, 1984, at the Lyndonville fairgrounds.

Before this, the last recorded camp meeting at the grove was held in 1915. The Railroad Grove is now Powers Park, owned and operated by the Lyndonville Village Improvement Society.

W. IRVING POWERS ENVISIONED A PARK FOR ALL

Washington Irving Powers was born at West Burke on October 11, 1862. He worked in the telephone business in Manchester, New Hampshire, and then as manager of the Brooklyn telephone exchange in New York. It was probably through the telephone business that he met Theodore N. Vail and came to Lyndon in 1890 to become clerk and treasurer of Vail's Speedwell Farms. He also organized and managed the successful Lyndonville Creamery. This association owned and operated fourteen creameries in Vermont and New Hampshire, with a branch in Boston for handling its own products like cheese and butter. He was president of the Lyndonville Board of Trade and a trustee of Lyndon Institute.

In 1915, W.I. Powers willed $13,000 to the Lyndonville Village Improvement Society (VIS) in which his daughter, Theia Powers Watson, was an active member. Mr. Powers had started negotiations with the Boston & Maine Railroad for the grove but died before they were completed. Having foresight, he left the money to the VIS so it could purchase the twenty-five-acre grove, setting aside a $10,000 trust fund for the development and maintenance of a community park, known today as Powers Park.

Mr. Powers foresaw how much this piece of natural woodland would add to the attractiveness of Lyndonville when developed as a playground for children and a place of outdoor recreation and nature walks. He entrusted this work to the VIS because it was in line with what the society had been doing for so many years.

He also realized how much effort his wife, daughter and other ladies of the community had put into the betterment of the community through the Lyndonville Village Improvement Society. Parks in the village were their main focus in beautification projects, planting flowers and shrubs, and they had various fundraising events to carry this through. They also installed the lamps at Bandstand Park in 1913.

Playground equipment in the early days of Powers Park consisted of a climbing rope hung from a maple tree, a sandbox, three swings, teeters, a merry-go-round, horseshoes and archery. There was also badminton, volleyball and other games. In 1991, the old worn-out playground equipment was replaced when the Bicentennial Playground at Powers Park was built and dedicated during Lyndon's bicentennial, with generous donations by many local businesspeople. A marker there lists their names.

The summer program (by 1997) was in full swing at Powers Park—owned and operated by the Lyndonville Village Improvement Society—with swimming lessons in the pool, tennis lessons under playground director Oralie Lafaive, playground equipment to play on between lessons, twice-a-week reading and games by the Cobleigh Public Library and twice-a-week arts and crafts. The fee for the summer lessons was fifty dollars per child. About 225 youngsters were in the swimming or tennis programs that summer. Qualified teenagers acted as paid staff during this opportunity for summer jobs. Upward Bound students helped in the snack bar.

Brian Woods acted as director in the afternoons when, for a small charge, people used the pool and tennis courts. On weekends during the summer,

The bronze sign of Powers Park remembering Washington Irving Powers.

A Glance Back in Time

The pool at Powers Park.

different families or business groups used the park for picnics, reunions or company gatherings.

It is to Washington Irving Powers that the area people owe their thanks for Powers Park; above all, much is owed to the Lyndonville Village Improvement Society, which primarily maintains the park and runs the summer programs. It also takes hard work and effort to raise the funds necessary to supplement the fees needed to maintain the park and keep programs going for everyone during the eight weeks in the summer. The VIS long ago had to give up other projects, including the former Bemis Community House (now the Breslin Center), in order to run Powers Park for the community.

THE OLD LOG HOUSE

The old Pierce House, as it was known, was one of only two original houses on the land that later became Lyndonville. It was located on the site of the present Shattuck House, on the corner of Broad and South Streets. The other house is on the street we call Park Avenue. The railroad called it West Street; after the school was built, it was known as School Street for a while.

The March 20, 1885 *Vermont Union* said: "In the south part of Lyndonville stands an ancient landmark in the shape of a log house which was built in 'ye olden time' and has ever since been occupied by 'Grandpa' and 'Grandma' Pierce."

Although Mr. and Mrs. Pierce were urged by friends to leave the house, they stood firm in their wishes to stay there, preferring to die in the house that they had built and in which they had lived for so many years. "Grandma Pierce, almost 93, still lives there," said the *Union*.

Franklin Horatio Smith, "the Village Poet," wrote many poems, often humorous, about people and places in Lyndonville and other places where he lived. In 1960, Smith family members published a collection of his poems, including one called "The Log House." It tells the story of Grandpa and Grandma Pierce—how they cleared the spot, built the log house and wished to remain there until they died. "Happy we have been, the meadow here beside."

After Mr. Pierce died, Franklin Smith added another five stanzas to the four-stanza poem in which Grandma Pierce asks the old house to be spared: "Two relics of the past, the old log house and I." The story goes that Grandma Pierce was to stay in the house as long as she lived. "As long as memory lasts, that old log house we'll spare. / Yes, Grandma, when you're gone, That relic of old days, / We'll leave right there alone, / 'Till every log decays."

Remembering Lyndon

This old photo is a familiar one in Lyndonville.

Charles M. Chase, publisher of the *Vermont Union*, and William Fletcher (my great-uncle) kept up in their generation the family friendship that went back a generation, to about 1811. That is why they felt free to pick on each other; Chase used his paper to get in a few friendly digs at Fletcher, who had a drugstore in Lyndonville where he sold his photography.

Chase wrote in the September 18, 1885 *Union*: "W.H. Fletcher is still operating that old camera, his last triumph being to photograph the old log house at the south end of the village, so long occupied by Mr. (and Mrs.) Pierce. It is a capital picture and every resident of the Ville ought to buy one off the ex-postmaster. It will be cheaper to support him in this way than to send him 'over the hill to the poorhouse.'" The photo of the log house is apparently not Fletcher's—he moved to California later in 1885. This photo is a post card ("Made in Austria for F.E. Dwinell, Druggist, Lyndonville, Vt"), unless Fletcher's photo was used by the Austrian company.

Milo and Eunice Leach and family lived in the log house for a few years when my mother-in-law, Emma (Leach) Fisher, was a little girl. She told me that one day in 1889, she was told to take her little brother Hadley ("Had") and play up on the hill, then open land (in the vicinity of what is now Skyline Drive), and to "stay a long time." When they returned to the house, they found a baby brother, Densmore "Dick" Leach.

A Glance Back in Time

However, "[t]hat relic of old days" was not allowed to remain "'[t]ill every log decays." While the Leaches lived in the log house, Eugene Leach, age nineteen, died of typhoid fever in 1892. My mother-in-law said the house was condemned and was set to be burned. According to the *Union*, "the south end of the village was burned last Friday night. Incendiary, and no mourners. It was the first house in the locality, at least 75 years old."

The old landmark is "preserved" in a picture, one copy hanging in the town clerk's office and one in the Cobleigh Library, and many postcards of it still exist.

THE VILLAGE POET

Did you know that in the 1880s there was a Lyndonville man known as the Village Poet? His name was Franklin Horatio Smith.

In 1960, Elva S. Smith copyrighted a booklet called *The Village Poet, Franklin Horatio Smith*. Elva S. Smith was a daughter of the poet but the booklet was a family project. The others in the family were Edith L. Smith, George E.P. Smith, Bertha Annette Smith and George E.P. Smith Jr. It was not offered with the idea of presenting "great poetry," they said, but rather with the feeling that the poems "depict in an interesting and entertaining way, some of the life and events of Lyndonville and northern Vermont in the 1880s."

Franklin Horatio Smith was born in Burke Hollow on July 18, 1841. His parents had lived on a farm in East St. Johnsbury and had just moved to Burke Hollow; here his father, Philip Smith, built and operated the local carding and fulling mill on the Passumpsic River. Carding and fulling are processes used in the manufacture of cloth.

The booklet says that Franklin's educational advantages came from the church in Burke Hollow, the one-room school, the daily family Bible at home and later the Newbury Seminary in Newbury, Vermont. He married Hattie Lovina Powers in January of 1868, and opened a small clothing goods store in Burke. In a few years, he had a successful clothing goods store in Lyndonville, later adding sewing machines, carriages and sleighs.

He was interested in the activities and politics of the village. He must have been born with a sense of rhyme. His keen wit and humor produced many poems concerning life in the village. He also liked to camp in the countryside and forests. He became a close friend of Charles M. Chase, editor and publisher of the *Vermont Union* at Lyndon Corner; many of Smith's poems were published in this paper.

Franklin Horatio Smith—"the Village Poet."

A Glance Back in Time

This is the "Fountain Lady" who "alight[ed] on our new-made park."

His poem "Ye Editor" pokes fun at Mr. Chase.

>*Ye Editor is a portly man, with brazen face and bold.*
>*'Tis said his ample stomach can*
>*A mighty dinner hold*
>*He walketh up and down the streets*
>*With pencil on his head,*
>*And pumpeth every man he meets*
>*Until that man is dead.*

One poem, called "The Public Square," refers to what today we call Bandstand Park. He speaks of the flowers, but also of the "beauty of our tater patch." It is true that part of the park was once planted with potatoes.

In a later poem, he writes of oats growing on the park.

>*The fountain lady looks around in deep surprise and pain.*
>*Before, she never was background to such a field of grain.*
>*But now, economy, you know, is ruling for a while;*

It ends with

> *We have no time, or taste, for praising*
> *The flowers that smell so sweet,*
> *For we must keep that park araising*
> *Something we can eat.*

"The fountain lady" figure is the feature in the poem, "Romance of Our Lady." It is about the large iron fountain that once graced the park. In its early days, the fountain was topped with a draped lady and a swan. The poet writes of a romance—a lover kissing the lady's cheeks "as cold as death." She "spurned him and steered her bark…Alighting on our new-made park, upon an iron bowl." And there she stood for many years "in sunshine and in storm / Pouring water o'er her form / To wash that kiss away." Eventually, the lady was taken down when village crews believed her to be too heavy for the fountain.

One of Smith's longer poems describes the controversy that arose when the village trustees and others wanted to build a village hall; some voters thought having the town hall at Lyndon Center was good enough.

For those that were for it, Smith wrote, "He may bawl, bawl, bawl, bawl, Village hall, Village hall!" Some voters thought that instead of spending money for a hall, "We'd like the sewers in the street to be a great deal more complete." The hall was built in 1884 and became a cultural and entertainment center. In the end, a shoe factory leased it and it burned down in 1953.

"Ho! Lyndon" is a political poem. "That Message" is a poem in reference to the Passumpsic Railroad, and "The Log House" is about the Grandma Pierce house that once stood, even before there was a Lyndonville, on a piece of land that became the corner of South and Broad Street. It was still there for a long time after the railroad built Lyndonville. A picture of the log house hangs in the Cobleigh Public Library.

The poet's wife died in 1882, leaving four young children. A few years later, Smith moved to California, where he helped lay out and organize South Pasadena. He wrote poetry about that area too. He built a hotel on Lyndon Street and planned to name it Marengo, but it burned down right after the grand opening and before anyone occupied it. Smith died of tuberculosis on October 9, 1889.

Franklin Horatio Smith's poetry is of historical significance to Lyndonville and the area because his poems were about the people and events here.

THE COMMUNITY BUILDING— CORNER GARAGE

Probably there is no building on Depot Street in Lyndonville that has had so many diverse activities to its credit than what we used to call the Corner Garage. It was named the Community Building when first constructed and it said so on a brick parapet or elevation on top of the building in the front. That sign is gone now. The block was generally referred to as the Corner Garage; the whole building at first was David (D.I.) Grapes's Corner Garage.

The building, now known as the Lang Block, has housed on the ground floor: the garage business first, two grocery stores (Grand Union and then First National), Toombs' Village Gift Shop, a newspaper publisher, a sandwich and soup shop and probably more. Upstairs has been car storage, a miniature golf course, a ballroom, an American Legion meeting hall, a shoe shop and perhaps more. There was a candlepin bowling alley in the basement.

The block was built by a group of subscribers, Grapes among them. Mr. Grapes had come from Charleston, Vermont, and started the Depot Garage across the tracks from the railroad station about 1915. He also bought Hotel Lyndon (the former Webb's Hotel).

The Community Building, a two-story brick block, took the place of the Stern and Eaton Blocks that burned on November 21, 1924. Across the street another building, known as the Realty Block, took the place of the Ide, Nichols and Masonic Blocks that had fallen in the same fire. You can't see the Realty name on this block any more either, probably because it is now privately owned.

The former Webb's Hotel that burned next to the Eaton and Stern Blocks was replaced by the Darling Inn, now a residence for seniors. All these new buildings were modern-style brick, except for the Darling Inn,

The Corner Garage, with its easy access from both streets. *Courtesy of Merlyn Courser.*

which was Colonial style; they all resulted from an energetic flurry—not only the reconstruction of that large portion of Depot Street, but an energetic community spirit as well. Farsighted people pooled their resources, their ideas and a sense of pride in making Lyndonville even better for work and play.

A large, lighted vertical sign on the Corner Garage proclaimed "Studebaker" and "Reo" in big letters. There was a Mobile sign with Pegasus, which we kids preferred to "the flying horse." A large sign on the corner near the bank on the Broad Street side said "Firestone" vertically and "Tires" horizontally. The handy thing about the service station part in those days was that cars could be driven into and out of it from either Broad or Depot Streets in the two service lanes.

There was a classy showroom on the first floor. Cars were driven in from an enclosed ramp on the side. In back was an enclosed elevator to take cars to the showroom upstairs; it was later used for car storage. It was fun to see the handsome new cars through the showroom windows from the street, but it was even more fun when your father and mother took you with them when they went in to browse. My parents bought Fords, usually from D.I.'s son, Forrest "Wild Trader" Grapes, who would bring a new model up to the farm and let us try it out to see if we were ready to trade.

A Glance Back in Time

The upstairs showroom of the Corner Garage. *Courtesy of Charlie Lang.*

In a 1929 *Union-Journal* ad, the Corner Garage promoted Studebakers. A President Eight sold from $1,735 to $2,350; the lowest-priced Studebaker was an Erskine Six, for $860 to $1,045. The difference in price no doubt depended on size and options. Other makes of automobiles may have been sold as well.

The area that is now the Green Mountain bookstore was formerly a grease pit, the Mobil Lubtritorium. Between that and the two aisles for the gas pumps was an area where small parts, such as spark plugs, were available. The office was in that section as well.

Eventually, the service garage part became Crandall's Service. Jack Cassady worked for Crandall's for a time, and then he took it over and it became Cassady's Mobile Station. The Grand Union store opened in the former showroom about 1940, Charlie Lang remembers.

The main room upstairs was made into a miniature golf course and was decorated by U.S. Grant in October of 1930. O.D. Mathewson, principal at Lyndon Institute, drove the first ball for the opening ceremonies; the course became busy immediately afterward. The proprietor, D.I. Grapes, thanked Mr. Mathewson for coming to take part in the ceremony. The course was busy until after midnight. Seats were provided for spectators. A sunset scene and a Willoughby Lake scene were painted on the walls by Gerald Flanders.

The upstairs showroom became a miniature golf course in 1931 and then the Sunset Ballroom in 1933.

A large, bordered advertisement in the *Vermont Union-Journal* invited all children under age fifteen to be guests of D.I. Grapes on Friday afternoon, October 17, and to play free of charge at the Sunset Indoor Miniature Golf Course. An instructor would show them how to play and parents were invited to come and watch.

Par for the miniature course was forty-one strokes. The first write-up in the *Union-Journal*, October 15, 1930, stated that Francis Hebert was the only one who had scored forty-one so far. Some others were listed in the low forties; and Mrs. Kenneth Aldrich was listed at forty-eight.

Mr. Grapes's son, Clarence, tended the miniature golf course and then the ballroom and the bowling alley, which opened about 1939. Quite some time later, Clarence went to Willoughby Lake to manage the Grapes's holdings there—cabins, a dance hall and a restaurant—and the Mountain Maid motor launch. "Wild Trader," as Forrest Grapes liked to be called, went into a car business in St. Johnsbury.

It may be that dancing seemed to be more popular than miniature golf. The golf course was taken out and replaced by the Sunset Ballroom, which many people around today still remember. H. Guy Dunbar's orchestra played for the opening dance on February 11, 1933. A set of iron stairs out back led to the entry where D.I.'s wife, Gracie, tended to the tickets and checked coats. (A more detailed account of the ballroom appears in *Hometown Album* under the heading, "Swinging in the Sunset.")

The basement was the Sunset Bowling Alley, opened about 1939. It closed in 1979. Bowling was a lot of fun. There were teams, both men's and women's. There were league plays and tournaments. (My mother and I were on different teams and even got to play against each other in tournaments). You sat on benches between turns to play. Also, there were benches behind these where people could sit to watch and cheer, or jeer, as the case might be. A gutter ball didn't produce many cheers unless they were cheering for the other side. I believe there was a pool table there also. There was a lunch counter where sodas, gum, chocolate bars, potato chips and more were available.

After the First National closed the grocery market, Mr. and Mrs. Toombs opened the Village Gift Shop. Later, Western Auto moved in from its other location on Depot Street to the larger quarters in the Lang Block in the 1970s.

Charlie and Erma (Grapes) Lang tried to have dances in the ballroom for a while in the 1950s, but the old dance orchestras were gone. A new and different type of music was the style and the crowds began to get somewhat rowdy, so the Langs gave them up. Charlie pumped gas for a while at the service station after the Cassadys left, but it became more difficult for cars to come in to the pumps and out to the other street as traffic increased. The open sides were closed in and what was the gas-pump area became part of the Western Auto store (now Shear Sensations Salon and Spa).

Green Mountain Books and Prints is presently located on the Broad Street side, over the former grease pit. Shear Sensations and Wayne's Appliances are located on the Depot Street side where the First National grocery was. For a time, Norman Silbernagel's *Weekly* newspaper office was on the west end; Lois Lang ran a collectibles and antique shop at that location for a while. Other businesses have rented that space from time to time.

ENTERTAINMENT WAS JUST AROUND THE CORNER

There were a lot of places to go for entertainment right in the center of Lyndonville in the thirties and forties. Those places are now gone or have changed to something else. Many people have enjoyed a lot of hours dancing or bowling in the Community Building.

You won't find the Community Building by that name any more. The name was on the brick extension running lengthwise across the top of the block facing Depot Street. That was taken down long ago, no doubt from fear of it falling on someone, and also the block has long been privately owned. The block was known by a more familiar name, the "Corner Garage," and was written up in the July 10, 1996 *Lyndon Independent* with a photo of the building.

The Sunset Miniature Golf course opened in 1931, upstairs in the Corner Garage block, and was fun for a time. The name "Sunset" was from the painting of a sunset over Willoughby Lake on the wall. In 1933, the golf course was replaced by a more popular entertainment—dancing in the Sunset Ballroom. The golf course floor had been built over to make one of the best dance floors in northern Vermont. There was ballroom dancing on Friday nights for a long time, with H. Guy Dunbar and His Versatile Band serving as orchestra. Other popular dance bands have played there. There were special balls held on New Year's Eve and Washington's Birthday. On Saturday nights the music was provided by Cedric "Ceddy" Sherrer, bouncing on the piano stool, his fingers dancing on the keys. He and his band offered a mix of lively round and square dances.

The Sunset Bowling Alley in the basement (it also had a sunset painted on the wall) was popular for a long time. It was candlepin bowling. As there were men's and women's leagues, it was busy most every night. Those were the days when the pin setters were boys and not automatic machines. I was on the team called "Anne Amateurs." I was an amateur all right—never got big scores—but we had a lot of fun. When my team bowled against my mother's team, she and I got a kick out of that.

Often there was something going on in Music Hall, just down Broad Street—roller skating, a music or a dance recital, maybe something hilarious like donkey basketball, something serious such as a well-known speaker, perhaps a graded school graduation or a Lyndon Institute graduation; Governor of Vermont George D. Aiken was the speaker at my own graduation, for instance.

Another choice for entertainment was just around another corner at the Gem Theater on Elm Street, where those Hollywood stars performed in wonderful "talkies." There were the Florenz Ziegfeld extravaganzas, musicals—who can forget *Rose Marie* with Jeanette MacDonald and Nelson Eddy—dramas, comedies and westerns. Sometimes there were local talent shows on the stage. The westerns were my dad's favorites, and sometimes when it wasn't haying time (so he could get milking done a little earlier), he and I went to Gene Autry westerns. On Saturday nights, the way it worked was that there was a double feature—a western and another movie. Dad and I got there in time for the second feature; the first feature was shown again, so we got to see both movies.

Depending on the season of course, there was the lighted skating rink, around the corner and down on Center Street. This is the spot where for many years, until 1933, a huge tent was set up in August for a week of culture and entertainment brought to Lyndonville by that traveling group known as Redpath Chautauqua.

Around another corner, from mid-June to mid-August, kids are seen romping in Bandstand Park while grown-ups sit on blankets or lawn chairs to hear the outdoor band concert by the Lyndonville Military Band.

Other entertainment and fun was available just outside the village in those days, too. It was only about two miles to Lyndon Outing Club (when it was in the Baril pasture), where there was a lighted slope, a rope tow and a warming cabin with a snack bar. The Lyndon Golf Club was a regulation nine-hole golf course in the Fletcher pasture, with fenced-in greens to keep the cows out. It was just up the hill from the village, near enough to play a round after work. I don't know when skeet shooting was first held in that pasture, but for a long time the cement-lined pit was still there where they threw out the clay pigeons. The funny thing was that neighborhood children and children from the village often played in the pasture, but I never heard of anyone falling into the pit. Probably nobody thought to tell us not to play there, so we didn't think of it. But I do remember seeing someone shooting at clay pigeons that were catapulted into the sky by someone in the pit.

A Glance Back in Time

Band concert night in Lyndonville. *Courtesy of the 1982 Community Calendar.*

Another place for entertainment near the village was the old Trotting Park that had become the Lyndonville Fairgrounds. It hadn't been used for several years, but in 1930 it was reactivated, the racetrack was restored and fairs (like Lyndonville Community Fairs) were held once again, with harness racing, agricultural competition, stage shows, rides, carnival games and more. In 1938, the Caledonia County Fair, long held in St. Johnsbury but closed for a few years, came to our fairgrounds, called Mountain View Park.

At some time in the 1950s, the Old Corner Boarding House on Depot and Main Streets was taken down and another movie house called the Plaza Theater took its place. I don't remember when the Gem Theater on Elm Street closed. I think the Gem and the Plaza operated simultaneously for a while. The Plaza entrance was under a marquee on Depot Street. The Plaza Theater is now the White Market, after many changes.

DANCING THE NEW YEAR IN

Three! Two! One! Midnight! Everyone shouts "Happy New Year!" H. Guy Dunbar's dance orchestra swings into "Auld Lang Syne." The Sunset Ballroom is filled with streamers, bursting balloons and noisemakers. The silver ball turns and glitters as 750 merrymakers—the largest crowd ever gathered at one place in the village of Lyndonville—dance their way far into the first morning of 1936.

People came to that dance from as far away as Newport, Derby, Lebanon, Littleton, Burlington, Montpelier and Barre. Parking was at a premium on Depot and Broad Streets, reported the newspaper on January 1, 1936. The *Vermont Union-Journal* kept its weekly schedule, even on a holiday, reporting that there were people on the street all night, a little noisy, but orderly, with "no unpleasant disturbances" of any kind. The restaurants were well patronized.

That same night, a New Year's party was in full swing at the Darling Inn, next door to the Community Building with the Sunset Ballroom upstairs. Seventy people celebrated at the inn until 5:00 a.m. A "splendid turkey dinner" was served from 10:00 p.m. until midnight. There was "excellent music," but the paper did not report who furnished the music. This New Year's celebration was an "annual custom and every year getting more hilarious," said the *Union*.

The New Year's Ball in Music Hall ushering in 1932 was termed "a perfect dance." The color scheme ranged from pink to the deeper American Beauty rose, with lights casting a soft glow and music by the popular Dunbar orchestra. Even the weather was ideal, mild and pleasant. The ninety couples stayed until the last strains of the orchestra died away.

The December 29, 1932 holiday ball at Music Hall was not a success, but not for the lack of the excellent music of Dunbar's orchestra or for the beautiful decorations that adorned the hall. Colored lights, red and green festoons, a large, lighted Christmas tree at the back of the hall and another on the stage certainly provided a holiday air. It was the weather—"the worst up to that time"—that put a crimp in the holiday spirit, causing those who did come to "one-step, two-step, and side-step" on the icy way to the door.

THE VILLAGE HALL WAS A CULTURAL CENTER

For a long time the Village Hall, also known as Music Hall, was the cultural and recreational center of Lyndonville. Before the Sunset Ballroom opened in February 1933, dances were held in Music Hall, built in 1884 and located on Broad Street (now the site of Post Office 05851). From the balcony, with its handsomely curved and decorative balustrade, those who did not wish to dance could watch the festivities below. The holiday dances were sponsored by the Lyndonville Village Improvement Society. This organization sponsored other dances and fundraising entertainments through the years. Decorating committees made the hall festive and beautiful. The New Year's Ball, or Holiday Dance as it was advertised, lasted from 9:00 p.m. to 1:00 a.m.

Before the decision was made to build the hall, there were mixed feelings around the village of Lyndonville in 1883. Some thought it unnecessary and that it would be a large expense and a luxury. Others, including village trustees William H. Fletcher, Stephen Eastman and Austin Houghton, thought it would be an advantage to have a village-owned place where large gatherings could meet in safety and comfort—a place for musicals, religious gatherings, political conventions, concerts, lectures, dramatics and more. There were meeting rooms upstairs in some of the blocks in Lyndonville and there was the Town House at Lyndon Center, but no place for such ambitious purposes as the pro-hall people thought would be good for the village—no space to call frequent audiences into the place, each hopefully leaving a little money and carrying away a good deal of advertising for the village.

"What voters seem to dread is letting go of the money. After they let go and obtain the improvement they will not sell at any price," wrote Editor Chase.

From left: Music Hall, Twombly's attractive four-tenement house and Twombly's store. The C&PRR passenger station is in the foreground, and behind it is Fletcher's block.

Franklin Horatio Smith wrote a poem—just in fun, he said, and not meant to offend anyone. The first verse goes:

> *Ring the bells with might and main,*
> *Rouse the people dull and lazy,*
> *Half the Ville has gone insane,*
> *Half the rest are going crazy,*
> *And they bawl, bawl, bawl, bawl,*
> *"Village Hall!" "Village Hall!"*
> *Up and down the street they go,*
> *Upon every voter call,*
> *Striving very hard to show*
> *How we need a village Hall.*

Trustees Fletcher and Eastman had purchased a hand-cranked, horse-drawn fire engine complete with one hundred feet of hose, a hose carriage and nozzles in Franklin, New Hampshire, in June of 1883. The engine soon arrived in Lyndonville, but the problem was that there was no place to house it. Why not build a village hall and make a place in it for the engine?

The trustees were given the go-ahead at the village meeting in 1884, and the cost was not to exceed $4,000. Fletcher and N.P. Lovering, looking for ideas, visited modern public halls in New Hampshire and Massachusetts.

The hall was begun right away. The foundation for the large wooden structure was fifty by ninety feet. A complete description appears on page

A Glance Back in Time

120 in the town history, *Lyndon, Gem in the Green*. The work of building the hall fell under the direction of the three trustees, with Fletcher as chief designer and Houghton as boss of the workmen.

At the front of the building, facing Broad Street, a person went up ten or twelve steps to two doors leading into the anteroom. Two doors led into the main hall and two sets of doors, one at each end of the anteroom, led up to balconies. The balconies were ornate, with wood and iron railings that gracefully curved outward enough to allow room for the knees of people sitting in the front row. The balcony at the end, facing the stage directly, was extended back over the entry and was reached by a series of steps from the side balconies.

As the balconies were self-supporting, no posts were needed underneath to the floor, leaving the whole floor free for dancing, bazaars and even for donkey basketball or roller skating in later years. Fletcher had also invented seats that could be folded back, were comfortable and were attached in rows so that a whole row could be pushed to the back of the hall (inside it was the back, outside it was the front) underneath the end balcony. I remember one fundraising donkey basketball game in which Kermit Grant and others kept us laughing all evening. At one point, "Shorty" Ramsdell had trouble with the donkey he was riding. Shorty just put his feet on the floor and the donkey walked out from under him.

The basement held a kitchen, dining room, police room, two lockups, wood room, furnace room, water closets and the fire engine room. At times, the lockups held those who needed to sober up overnight.

The main hall was fifty by sixty feet. The stage was three feet above the floor, with a recessed area for footlights, an arch for drop curtains and space in the rear for sliding in scenery. There were dressing rooms beyond each end of the stage.

There were all kinds of gatherings and entertainment in that building—musicals, concerts, lectures, conventions, plays, dances, balls (a Washington's Birthday ball was held each year for fifty years), bazaars, movies, graded school graduations and Lyndon Institute graduations.

There were minstrel shows held before they offended anybody. Everybody just had a lot of fun. There were union services on the Sunday before Memorial Day. People came from Boston and directed local talent in plays and musicals. The Lyndonville Military Band held concerts one winter because we were raising money for new uniforms.

Radio and automobiles are considered responsible, in great part anyway, for the eventual lack of interest in the cultural events and entertainment in Music Hall. The State of Vermont rented it for use by Company C of the National Guard, but it could still be rented for local use. Basement rooms

A girl's dancing class show, apparently the Fourth of July. *Courtesy of Margaret Randall.*

Band concert in Music Hall, raising money for new uniforms; the director is Perley Harris and the singer is Wanda Sheldon. Harriet Fletcher is second row from right, front. 1940.

continued to be the offices and stockroom of the Lyndonville Electric Company. A garage at the end of the sloping driveway was used by the electric company for company trucks. The Village Improvement Society, which used the building for many fundraising activities, built a portico for the front steps.

The village bought the Gem Theater on Elm Street, converted it to an armory and remodeled the village hall, making another floor at balcony level. The village leased those two floors to the Vermont Shoe Company in 1953.

On October 23, 1954, the building that had seen so much activity for so many years burned to the ground. The story was told that a glue pot used in the shoe manufactory had been left on all night, causing it to overheat and start the fire.

Today the large wooden building would have been considered a detriment, unsafe and impossible to insure. But for many years, it served as a social center as well as a center for village meetings for Lyndonville and the surrounding area.

ANTIQUES & EMPORIUM
182 S. WHEELOCK RD.
LYNDONVILLE, VT 05851
(802) 626-3500

Date: 6/28/05

Reg. No.	Clerk	Account Forward		
1	LYNDONBOOK	N	16	00
2			TAX 9	7
3			17	17
4				
5				
6				
7				
8				
9				
10				
11				
12				
13				
14				
15				

Your Account Stated to Date - If Error is Found, Return at Once

THANK YOU
Call Again

We appreciate your patronage and
hope we may continue to merit it.
If we please you, tell your friends.
If we don't, tell us.
We strive to satisfy.

THE MASONIC BUILDING

The subject of fire comes up quite frequently in the history of Lyndonville village. The fire of November 30, 1894, destroyed both sides of Depot Street; in the rebuilding, the Masonic Order formed an association to erect a building of its own. The handsome Masonic Block resulted, but had a short life—from 1895 to January 21, 1924.

Masonic officers at the time were Theodore N. Vail, president; James T. Gleason, vice president; and Fred E. Dwinell, S.B. Hutchins and Walter E. Ranger, directors. All of those names are familiar in the village history. The block was built by day labor under the direction of Dwinell, on the site of the burned three-story Nichols Block at the corner of Depot and Church Streets.

Under the corner ornament on the block is the date "1895." Under the ornament to the right of it are the words, "Masonic Building." Just above a window in front hangs an electric light. A wire to the electric light stretches from across the street.

History can be read or verified with magnifying glasses. This brings out many details in some old photos that I have found. I discovered the following by examining an old photo of the Masonic Block: The corner store is Edmunds, and above the window at the left side of the door it said, "Druggists, school supplies, soda, cigars." On the window under the awning are the words, "Stationery and rubber goods." Also on the window is the word "Kodak." Above the window on the right it said, "Druggists, toilet articles, Kodaks, supplies," and under the window it says, "Fishing tackle, sporting goods."

At the next store, "Dexter Jeweler" appeared on the upper half of part of the window, with "Watch repairs" appearing underneath. The other part of the window read, "Campbell & Blodgett, coal, insurance." This business office took up half the room and Dexter's store took up the other half.

The 1895 Masonic Block housed many businesses. You could check the time in front of the Dexter jewelry store. The block stood almost thirty years between two fires, 1894 and 1924.

Jim Dexter, jeweler, shows a clock to a customer while Blodgett waits for customers in his insurance office in his half of the store.

A Glance Back in Time

The corner store at the right of the Masonic building was "Lapoint Brothers." On the window of the door was "Salada" and "Pure Food Service." Apartments, offices and a barber shop were on the second floor. The telephone office was probably upstairs then because the Bell telephone sign hung above the middle entrance. There would have been a meeting hall on the top floor.

The photo I examined was taken at 8:27 a.m. according to the clock—shaped like a huge watch—that hangs over the doorway to Dexter's jewelry store. Between the Dexter/Campbell & Blodgett door and Lapoint's door is one that leads upstairs. The three doors are in a recessed area. Just above the clock, three barber poles jut out from that three-window section.

In the street, near an automobile on the left, is a post with what looks like a kerosene lantern on top. Traffic at this intersection was warned by the wording on the post, "Keep to right." Parking was apparently no problem at 8:27 a.m.

A pickup truck is parked on the other side of the automobile on the right—one can see the back-left wheel of the truck beyond the automobile. It would be interesting if someone could identify the two cars, as I could not. The white box on the posts at the left of the building may have contained electric meters. There is a utility pole in front of the automobile at the left.

It is amazing what history one can find with an old photo and a magnifying glass!

The Realty Block of today replaced two—the Masonic and Ide Blocks—that burned in a fire on January 21, 1924. Some of the businesses relocated to the newly built Realty Block, including Dexter's jewelry and watch repair shop, still sharing unpartitioned space with Campbell & Blodgett, which at some point became Blodgett & Hopkins.

James D. Dexter, who ran the jewelry store in the Realty Block, once told me a story about one of his customers. He knew I would appreciate the story because I knew the customer. He was my father's cousin, Fred Chesley, a very moderate man. Like most moderate people, he accomplished a lot because no movement was wasted and he made sure he was doing it right in the first place.

Mr. Dexter told the story this way:

> *Fred comes into my store one day and stands there looking at watches in the showcase. I am seated at my work bench repairing a watch. I greet him, but keep right on working. You didn't hurry Fred, you know. After quite a while, Fred says, "May I see that watch?" and points to a particular one. I get up, take the watch out and lay it on top of the case.*

I go back to my work. You didn't hurry Fred, you know. Fred looks the watch over for a while. After some minutes, Fred asks, "How much is this watch?" I get up, look at the watch and tell him the price. I go back to work. You didn't hurry Fred, you know. Fred still studies the watch. I am still working. After a while, Fred says, "I'll take it."

THE JOURNEY OF THE COVERED BRIDGE

In July of 1960, the Sanborn Bridge between Lyndonville and Lyndon Center traveled upstream to a different location. Well, it didn't actually travel upstream. It took to the road in a roundabout way along Center Street and the length of Main Street. It had help from a crew of men, rollers and a heavy hauler; a lot of onlookers cheered them on.

While Dr. Venila Shores, official Lyndon historian, was working on Lyndon history, she went back to the early days of each of our five covered bridges to settle on the most appropriate historic names once and for all. Bridge names were often called by the name of the family living near them, which changed occasionally. Dr. Shores believed that the Center Bridge should be called Sanborn again because the Sanborns lived in the house on the east side of it and the bridge was not exclusive to Lyndon Center (on one side of it, while Lyndonville was on the other).

A new concrete bridge was being built to replace the covered bridge. Armand Morin, owner of the Lynburke Motel, and Herbert Gallagher "pooled their resources," as Herb said, and bought the covered bridge for $1. Herb Gallagher laughed about this one. They paid $1 for the bridge and spent $5,000 to move it, he said. The point of saving the bridge was that it was too good to destroy, Herb said, and it was sort of a venture.

The bridge was built about 1858, when a road was made across this meadow connecting Lyndon Center with farms on the eastern side of the Passumpsic. There was no Lyndonville then, and farmers in town had to go to Lyndon Center or Lyndon Corner for needs from stores or other business.

The bridge, of Paddleford construction (a highly regarded way of building a covered bridge), is considered one of the best examples in the state. Herb Gallagher and Mr. Morin set about finding someone to move it. On some

The covered bridge makes its way slowly up Main Street to a new location.

photos of the moving of the bridge you can read on the side of the truck, "J.M. Giddings, Industrial & Heavy Hauling, Springfield, Vt."

One difficulty was getting the bridge off of its original site. Every time sand was dumped, on which they would slide the bridge off of its abutment, it rained and the sand washed it away. It may have been a rainy summer because it took quite a long time before things were finally ready to get the bridge started on its journey. Logs, or rollers, were placed under the bridge, and with the hauler truck in front it was time to get moving.

As the bridge made its way slowly along Center Street and came to the corner of Main Street, where Guibord's Funeral Home is now, something had to be done about a tree that hampered the progress of turning the bridge around that corner. Herb suggested digging around the roots so the tree could be bent over, worked and lifted back into its upright position after the bridge went. No doubt these people had done this kind of heavy hauling before.

From that corner, as the bridge came off Center Street and onto Main Street, the rest of the way up Main Street was straight. Linemen went ahead to unhook lines and then put them back after the bridge passed by.

It was a slow process, though, and the bridge stayed one night on Main Street to resume its journey in the morning. When it finally reached its

A Glance Back in Time

destination over the Passumpsic River behind Lynburke Motel, it seemed to settle nicely into its new home.

Though there had been some thought of making it a tearoom or a gift shop, closing it in would have taken away from the bridge's beauty and this did not come about. Gerald Farrington rented space, built a small, separate shelter inside and used it for an office for his real estate business for quite some time. The bridge has also been used for "yard" sales, a unique setting for such sales and an opportunity to visit a covered bridge and look over the construction closely from the inside.

Between the rent from Farrington and selling the bridge to Arthur Elliott at Lynburke Motel, "We made out all right," or at least came out even, Herb said.

Many people like to see all five of our covered bridges, and the old Center or Sanborn Bridge at LynBurke Motel is one of them. In its original place, the bridge carried lots of people across the river to work and other places. Any of us going to Lyndon Institute from the Lyndonville side of the bridge walked through it twice a day and five days a week for several months of the year.

With five covered bridges in town, Lyndon claims to be the Covered Bridge Capital of the Northeast Kingdom. *Courtesy of the* Lyndon Independent.

THE GREENING OF THE GEM

Sergeant Joyce Kilmer, born December 6, 1886, and killed in action near Ourcy on July 30, 1918, wrote the poem "Trees" that so many of us learned in our school days. A final question on *Jeopardy!* recently asked for the poem containing the line, "A nest of robins in her hair." I knew that one immediately and as I thought about the poem, I was surprised by how much of it I remembered. If trees are poetry, a lot of it is going on in Lyndonville these days. It began a few years ago, when the Japanese lilacs were planted along Depot Street. These trees blossomed profusely this year.

In the months of 1998, remarks passed around that the trees, necessarily taken down the previous year or so because of age or storm damage, were quite missed. Soon the "Greening of the Gem" project was born. The committee includes Ellen Doyle, Paula Gaskin, Elaine Bixby, Harriet Fisher and tree consultant Steve Elliott of Elliott's Greenhouses and Landscaping.

Careful consideration was taken to make sure planted trees would not interfere with underground facilities or grow too near overhead wires. The village trustees approved the plan and municipal assistant David Dill had the village crew mark the spots for the new trees. The Lyndon Area Chamber of Commerce and the Lyndon Historical Society endorsed the greening plan. The idea of making it a memory tree planting project soon took hold. To date, about twenty trees have been planted or pledged by individuals, families and organizations. Suitable trees in a varying price range include lindens, maples, flowering trees, oaks and elms.

In the 1860s, after the Connecticut & Passumpsic Rivers Railroad built the shops and all of the necessary facilities for that thriving business, a new village—Lyndonville—grew within the town of Lyndon. Not wanting the new village to turn into a "shack town," the railroad company laid out streets and building lots, reserved a place for a park and required lot buyers to build houses at least two stories high and no nearer than twenty feet to any street.

To add to the pleasant appearance of a new village, the railroad company planted elms and maples along the sides of the streets. Many of these died, but in 1884, the village set out about planting five hundred elms and maples. Two years later, two hundred more trees (balms of Gilead) were planted. "In both cases, Austin Houghton, street commissioner and village trustee served as the impetus, as he did in other village beautification projects," as described in the Lyndon history, *Gem In the Green*. People bragged about the beauty of Lyndonville's trees for many years, until the Dutch elm disease killed those lofty, impressive elms. Main Street especially was "an archway of elms."

Austin Houghton was born in 1839 on a farm in the Red Village area, where Nathan and Fran Houghton live today. Austin was great-uncle to Nathan and brother to Nathan's grandfather, Silas Houghton. Nathan and Fran are planting an elm tree in Bandstand Park in memory of Austin Houghton, who did so much to develop that park back in the 1880s. Potatoes had occasionally been planted in the park, and there was a time when part of it served as a dump. Austin Houghton lived across the street in a house that was taken down to make a larger parking lot for the White Market. Houghton died in 1912, so he had many years to enjoy the beautiful park, with its walks, fountain, bandstand, trees and flowers.

Houghton's elm tree graced Depot Street for many years.

A Glance Back in Time

Editor Charles M. Chase told a story about Austin Houghton in his paper, the *Vermont Union*. The elm tree on the small triangular park near the railroad station was called "Houghton's Tree." Chase reported that Houghton's tree was dead and a funeral would be held to mourn it. Not long after, Chase reported that "Houghton's tree lives and Houghton is happy." It makes me happy, too, to remember that beautiful elm that still stood on that spot not so many years ago. A photo of that tree appears in the June 3 *Lyndon Independent*, under "Lyndon Lore." The photo was taken before 1924, when some of the buildings shown burned down. There are other *Vermont Union* references to tree planting in Lyndonville and other areas in the town of Lyndon.

Under the greening project, trees have been planted in Memorial Park, South Street Park and on the Municipal Building grounds, as well as in other areas. Trees so far planted or pledged are in memory of Ralph Secord, Frederick "Ted" Tolman, Dr. John Mangus, Dean Parker, Warner Scribner (former trustee of Lyndonville), Herbert Gallagher and Susan Gallagher. The maple tree in memory of the Fletcher-Fisher families includes William H. Fletcher (my great-uncle), who was a village trustee along with Austin Houghton and Stephen Eastman; also included is Phineas S. Fisher, who quarried stone on Kirby Mountain, stone that was later used to build some

Todd Wellington and Ellen Doyle, the latter the instigator of the Greening of the Gem, carry a tree to be planted in memory of Hazen Russell by the river behind the municipal building, 1999.

of the foundations of houses in the new Lyndonville and one of the tombs at Lyndon Center cemetery.

Other trees have been planted by the Mothers Club and the Juniper Branch of Rebecca Lodge No. Nine; an elm on Elm Street was planted for the hundredth anniversary of St. Peter's Episcopal Church. A Japanese lilac was planted on the Cobleigh Public Library side lawn by patrons of the library, and one in memory of Tom Breslin was planted at the Tom Breslin Center. The tree planted on the Park Street Laundry lawn is in memory of Sergeant Fred Graves, who was a retired member of the state police.

A storm-damaged and aging tree was removed from Bandstand Park recently and another one or two must also come down soon. Happily, the Houghton elm and one planted by the Lyndon Woman's Club will help fill the gap. The Greening of the Gem project stopped after a while, only because all the requests and all the suitable places were filled.

CHRISTMAS IN LYNDONVILLE

No one seems to remember exactly when Lyndonville was first lighted for Christmas, but the opinion is that colored lights have been strung since the middle or late thirties. (I remember strings of colored lights hanging across Depot Street from building to building before the Crown of Lights appeared.)

How many people remember the little park on Depot Street near the railroad station? This little park, sort of triangular or oval-shaped, once had a tall, elegant elm tree. There was grass in the summer and an evergreen tree was strung with colored lights during the Christmas season.

Workmen from Lyndonville Electric would spot a likely Christmas tree when working on lines in the countryside. Come Christmastime, one was chosen, five dollars were given to the landowner for it and then it was installed complete with strings of colored lights. The tree was usually about forty feet tall and was a beautiful sight to greet visitors to the village and townspeople as well when they went "down, up, or over street," depending on which direction they came from.

Besides the tree, colored lights were strung across Broad and Depot Streets. At times there was a tree with electric lights on the Main Street Park. At first, a large pine tree growing naturally on the park was used for Christmas, but being of a flexible nature it seemed a little too dangerous for the men to be putting ladders against it for climbing (this was before the "cherry picker" facility). Then for a number of years, a tree was found, brought to the park and decorated with colored lights for Christmas.

Inevitably things change—bulbs were stolen from the trees at too costly a rate and the tree became a lost cause. The little park near the railroad in which automobiles could drive around—a sort of turnaround—was removed and the space became the parking lot that we see today. That ended having the Christmas tree on that spot.

Remembering Lyndon

After Houghton's elm tree died, the Lyndonville electric crew set a freshly cut and lighted Christmas tree every year.

A Glance Back in Time

For over forty years, the Nativity scene has been a familiar and greatly anticipated sight in Lyndonville. *Courtesy of Steve Legge.*

Some time ago, Lyndonville had an immense wooden star that was brought out from storage every year, covered with evergreen boughs and colored lights and placed high on the Norris Block (now Mathewson Block) facing into Depot Street. Later, a lighted Santa Clause with his bulging bag of toys looked down the length of the street from that point. The plastic Santa was much easier to put at the top of the building than the wooden star, which was of considerable weight.

Then in 1964, something new happened. "It's beginning to look a lot like Christmas." All over town, homes were aglow with colored lights and the promise of Christmas. The village of Lyndonville is displaying an unusual Christmas lighting arrangement this year. A huge crown, suspended over Depot Street and made of gleaming aluminum, glows with red and blue bulbs. Many strings of lights loop gracefully from the crown. The strings are lighted entirely with soft blue bulbs, in contrast to the multicolored lights of the other strings that have been placed across the streets at Christmastime for many years. One Friday in 1992, men from the Lyndonville Electric Plant worked all day in the icy rain to get the trees and the crown ready to light that evening.

The Lyndonville Electric Department gets the crown in place and energized before Christmas. *Courtesy of Jeanne Miles.*

"The Glow of Christmas." *Courtesy of Steve Legge.*

A Glance Back in Time

Paul Aubin, a Lyndonville jeweler, and Lee Gray, manager of Lyndonville Electric, designed the crown and all businesses in the "ville" donated money for the crown project; the funds were matched in the village.

Also new in Lyndonville that year were small evergreen trees, two on each streetlamp post. These trees were decorated with multicolored lights that blinked alternately. (A few years later, to save cutting natural trees and stringing lights on them each year, Paul Aubin reconstructed artificial trees with dowels and wires and permanent lights. They can be kept in storage as they don't need restringing each year.)

One year, the Grinch stole Christmas and Ebenezer Scrooge was in town—Bah Humbug!—in the form of an energy crunch. There were no colored lights whatsoever in the village streets. It was a bleak Christmas without so much as a big wreath of evergreens, which would have been welcomed. This was never repeated—the next year, lights again appeared on the street and the Christmas spirit returned to Lyndonville.

THE SNOWFLAKE

Did you notice the big snowflake suspended over Depot Street? It disappeared for a couple of years. In 2002, it reappeared in time for the Snowflake Festival.

The snowflake is the work of Paul Aubin, who is remembered by many as an individual of high community spirit; he was a jeweler, designer, musician and inventor. It was he who designed and made the snowflake some time in the 1980s. It may have been about 1985, which seems to be the first year of the now-traditional Snowflake Festival.

Suspended over Depot Street, it was made to enhance the spirit of the traditional winter carnival time—the Snowflake Festival, sponsored by both the Lyndon Area and Burke Chambers of Commerce, coincided with the annual (since 1937) Lyndon Outing Club Carnivals.

Paul Aubin's son, Peter, who lives in Florida said his father worked on the snowflake in his garage, using scrap aluminum, but he didn't remember what year he made it. He painted it white and added some glitter material so it would sparkle in the sun. The shapes of snowflakes were interesting to him and were among his many jewelry designs.

The village's electric department hangs the snowflake as it does the Christmas crown. The snowflake seems to have been overlooked for a year or two, so it was good to see it up again in 2002. It presided over a good snowfall just before the holidays that year, so the Lyndon Outing Club was able to have its carnival activities, torchlight parade and corporate cup race, all of which were well attended. And of course, Burke Mountain was doing very well, with record crowds and festival activities, according to newspapers.

Paul Aubin may have been a dreamer, but he thought his dreams through and made them come true through hard work and perseverance. He said that it may sound strange to say that having no money for toys when he

The snowflake, designed and created by Paul Aubin circa 1986, puts the carnival spirit into activities of the Burke/Lyndon Winter Festival.

was a boy was fortunate. It was fortunate, he said, because family members learned to make things and it was fun.

He said he and his brothers, David and Gerald, would go to the local fruit store and pick up empty fruit crates, which were free. Many crates had two sections, and some people covered them with fabric, making a curtain in front, and used them for two-shelf storage space.

The Aubin boys would take apart the crates they got and use the wood to make trucks, airplanes and other toys. This not only let them have a lot of fun using tools, but it also put their imaginations to use as well; it was the beginning of many other creative ideas that came to their minds.

One thing Paul liked to do was talk to youngsters about dreams. He wasn't talking about dreams in sleep, but dreams of when they might think of things to do or make, or maybe what they wanted to be when they grew up. He told them how he worked on his dreams.

Paul wanted to go to the Rhode Island School of Design in Providence. A friend, Harley Folsom, who was going to Brown University, found Paul a job waiting on tables in a restaurant in Providence. In order to pay his school expenses, Paul went without treats such as chocolate bars and so on, but he was working on his dream, and a year at the Providence School of Design was part of it.

A Glance Back in Time

After he finished his year in design school, he spent a summer in Taunton, Massachusetts, learning watch work. He then worked for a jeweler in St. Johnsbury for ten years.

When he started his own store, he began to realize his dream. He started small and kept adding things when he was able. As a jeweler, he designed and made many items from his own unique patterns, one of his favorites being snowflakes.

Many people remember when Paul's jewelry store was in the building with the blue awning on Depot Street. One thing he invented was a way to skip the bothersome task of running to get the long-handled crank and going outside to operate it every time he wanted the awning up or down (since the weather changed so often). He invented a way to do that job so that all he had to do was press a button in the store and his awning went up or down as he wanted.

Another very handy item he invented for his house was an outside elevator, with a motor and equipment in the basement. The elevator took him to the roof of his house. One day, when he went up to clear snow off the roof, the ladder slipped and he "almost broke [his] neck," he said. After he made the elevator, he liked to go up onto the flat roof, even to take a lawn chair up on a nice day to enjoy the view from up there. "It was the best place to see Lyndonville," he said.

It's so satisfying when you make something with your own two hands, Paul used to tell children. He would tell them not to be afraid to help people. "It makes you feel good inside, and the better you feel inside, the more you are going to accomplish."

When he was talking to a group of children in the Cobleigh Library on March 1, 1989, he talked about making the snowflake that they could see hanging over the street. "The snowflake took four and a half days to make," he said. "There was no money in it, but it was four and a half days of fun." He wanted the children to know that they don't have to get money every time for things they do.

"If you think of something you might like to try to make," he would tell the children, "don't be afraid to try it—it might come out even better than you think it will." He also suggested to them, "If you have a problem when you are trying to make something, first try solving the problem yourselves. Don't be afraid to dream and dream of how to realize your dream."

He told the group that day in 1989, "I am seventy-five. Every day is a challenge and I am never bored."

FAMILY DOCTOR OF AN EARLIER DAY

I remember going to Dr. Cheney's office in his house on Church Street when the school nurse suggested to my mother that she should have my tonsils checked. I suspect the "district nurse," as she was called, couldn't see them because she gagged me with that tongue depressor. My impression of Dr. Cheney was that he was a kind man in a gray suit, with gray hair and gray bushy eyebrows; to my relief, he always would say, "They look all right to me." I had heard of some of my schoolmates having their tonsils removed on a kitchen table, often used as an operating table back in those days, and it didn't appeal to me.

Albertus A. Cheney was born September 30, 1862, in Albany, Vermont, and attended Albany and St. Johnsbury Academies. Determined to become a physician, he read medicine with Dr. C.W. Dustan of Craftsbury, studied at Rush Medical College of Chicago and graduated in 1887 from the medical department of the University of Vermont. Dr. Cheney practiced his profession in West Burke for five years before coming to Lyndonville in 1892.

Wilmot R. Cheney, his younger brother from Albany, studied pharmacy. He took a job in Haverhill, New Hampshire, working as a shipping clerk in the Whetstone Manufacturing Company, an industry started by A.F. Pike that turned out grindstones and whetstones. Wilmot hoped to earn enough money to start a drugstore somewhere and pursue his profession. He married one of Pike's daughters, but when his daughter Evelyn (born in 1892) was about three and a half months old, his wife died. Evelyn's grandparents took her home to the Cheney farm in Albany, Vermont. Wilmot followed his dream, coming to Lyndonville in 1892, where he went into partnership with his older brother Albertus, opening a drugstore in the Weeks Block on Depot Street.

The Cheney brothers used this temporary shack for a store until the new brick block was built after the 1924 fire. W.D. Weeks held store in the right side of the building.

A 1893 advertisement in the *Vermont Union* reads, "Cheney Brothers Druggists. Fine drugs and chemicals, large line of albums, toilet cases, celluloid goods, diaries, and everything which goes with this line of trade. Prescriptions carefully compounded. Call here for a fine cigar and for your holiday goods."

The Cheney brothers lost everything in November of 1894, when the great fire leveled thirty-four businesses on Depot Street and several houses on Elm and Church Streets, including the fine house that Frank Silsby had built on Church Street (sold to a Mr. Twombly, who later sold it to Dr. Cheney for $4,250).

The people of Lyndonville were back in business almost immediately after the fire, finding places wherever they could, and several temporary buildings sprang up almost overnight, two of them on Church Street; one bore the sign, "Cheney Bros., Drug Store," and the other was Weeks's store and post office. Rebuilding began at once and in a couple of years a new Lyndonville appeared.

By February 8, 1896, a deed conveyed premises to the firm of Cheney Brothers for $8,000, from W.D. Poole, who had also lost a store in the fire. The Cheney brothers moved into their fine new store. In the new Cheney Block store were all the same drugs and goods that were sold as before, and it also had an elegant syrup soda fountain dispensing "temperance drinks."

A Glance Back in Time

Dr. Cheney built a new three-story Victorian house to replace the house he lost. Others have owned the house since Dr. Cheney. In recent years, it has been restored to its Victorian beauty. It is the second house on the left as you go north on Church Street.

Dr. A.A. Cheney was a familiar figure in and around Lyndonville for more than fifty years. Besides his professional work, he was also commissioner of the Lyndonville Electric Plant for many years. His signature, A.A. Cheney, was almost as familiar as the doctor himself.

Locally, Dr. Cheney was a member of Crescent Lodge, Free and Accepted Masons at the Lyndonville and St. Johnsbury chapter of Royal Arch Masons. In a wider area, he was a member of the Vermont State Medical Society, the Northeastern Medical Society and of the American Medical Association. His brother Wilmot was a member of the State Pharmaceutical Society and "a genial salesman," said the *Lyndonville Journal* on July 1, 1896. Dr. Cheney was fond of music and was a member of the Lyndonville Military Band. I don't know what instrument he played, but his grandson, Richard Cheney, has an undated photo of his grandfather with the band when he was director for a time. The doctor's son Paul, who was born in 1892, also played in the band.

Dr. Cheney, busy practicing his profession and caring for those who needed his medical skill, saw the advantage of having an automobile to make his trips to rural areas easier and speedier, perhaps except in snow and

Dr. Cheney's first car. He found that it didn't stop when he hollered "Whoa!"

mud seasons at first. "Soon after my grandfather purchased his first auto," Jack Cheney Jr. wrote in 1997, "it must have been hard to break old habits. My Uncle Maurice once told me that he watched as his father approached the garage at home in his auto, and as he went into the garage he was pulling back on the steering wheel and yelling, 'Whoa, damn it, whoa!' The result was that he demolished the sleigh at the rear of the garage before he was able to stop. Maurice remembered the incident well because he was supposed to have moved the sleigh from that location."

Evelyn Cheney Brooks comes into the story because of a paper she wrote about her life. When Evelyn was ready for high school, she moved from the Cheney farm in Albany to Lyndonville, where she lived in the home of her Uncle Bert (Dr. Albertus Cheney) and attended Lyndon Institute (LI). In Lyndonville, she became better acquainted with her father, Wilmot Cheney. At her uncle's house, she also got to know her cousins (Dr. Cheney's sons) Paul, Maurice and Jack. They became LI graduates—Paul in 1909, Maurice in 1912 and Jack in 1920. Paul was in Evelyn's class at LI, but she went on to LaSalle Seminary.

Evelyn wrote about her uncle's Victorian house. "To my country eyes, the house was palatial." Dr. Cheney was evidently as fond of good books as he was of music, for Evelyn wrote, "Its greatest asset was my uncle's books which I devoured." She read Victor Hugo, Walter Scott, Shakespeare and other authors, as well as political writings. At times she went with her uncle

Dr. Cheney's house, built after the fire, seemed "palatial" to his niece Evelyn.

when he made professional calls in the country. "Aunt Ida was always kind, though not affectionate," she wrote.

Her relationship with her father, whom she had seen only on visits before moving to Lyndonville, grew into a satisfying father-daughter relationship. Their short conversations when she passed through the store on her way to and from LI meant a lot to her. He took her to lectures, maybe at Music Hall, to a hotel for an occasional meal out and took an interest in her studies at Lyndon Institute.

In 1913, the Cheneys sold their space to A.W. Edmunds, who had a drugstore and soda fountain there for many years. Dennis Stevens owned the block and ran the drugstore for a long time, and then Robert Fichera was the owner before he moved to Florida. The present owner of the block, Vincent Matteis, has done much to restore the old Cheney Block. Fabrictown now occupies the former drugstore.

A.A. Cheney never retired. On the very last day of his life, August 22, 1942, he was still doctoring and took a patient to the hospital. Later, at home, he worked outside for a while and went in to take a nap. It was there that his housekeeper found him when she returned from shopping. He had died in his sleep. His wife, Ida Lyon Cheney, had died in 1935. I did not find out what happened to the doctor's brother, Wilmot.

Richard Cheney, the doctor's grandson from Connecticut, who sent the photos and Evelyn's autobiography to me, is Jack's son. Richard used to visit his grandfather in Lyndonville.

DR. VENILA LOVINA SHORES'S LEGACY

The Shores Memorial Museum was one of four landmarks on the list for preservation work and was a goal of the Lyndon Historical Society's fundraising campaign. Probably most everyone is familiar with the Shores Memorial Museum, but a recap of what the museum is and the woman whose home it was may remind us of what it means to Lyndon's heritage.

Venila Lovina Shores, who earned many academic degrees, "was also a handy woman with tools, hammer, hoe, pruning shears, egg beater, needle, pipe wrench and typewriter," said Florida State University colleague Dorothy Mayo Harvey. Shores was born on March 19, 1893, to James and Alla (Gage) Shores. They lived in Alla Shores's parents' house on Main Street in Lyndonville until James Shores built a house for himself, his wife and their little daughter at Lyndon Center about 1895. Dr. Shores never married and when she died in 1980, she bequeathed her home to the town of Lyndon for a museum.

Venila attended school at Lyndon Center and graduated from Lyndon Institute in 1910. She received her BA from Bates College in Maine, her MA at Smith College and her PhD at Johns Hopkins. She also received an honorary LittD degree from Bates.

Dr. Shores taught for a while in schools in Maine and Vermont, and then went to Florida State Teachers College for Women to help establish a demonstration school. She had been an active and leading figure in community affairs, including the American Association of University Women, the Woman's Club, the DAR, the Tallahassee Historical Society and many more. She was also, according to friend Dorothy Mayo Harvey, "A cut-throat bridge player in the Saturday Night Auction Bridge Club." Venila's many academic accomplishments are documented in *Who's Who in America* and other publications.

Remembering Lyndon

Above: Dr. Venila L. Shores.

Right: Venila L. Shores. Lyndon Institute graduation, 1910.

    She came back to Lyndon Center each summer and worked diligently on the history of the town of Lyndon. She was named the official town historian. After her retirement from Florida State University in 1957, she returned to Lyndon Center and continued to work on Lyndon's history, collecting data and old photos. She had begun the manuscript for publication, but died before it was completed. Ruth Hopkins McCarty, who grew up across the street from the Shores house, retired from teaching history in Connecticut, came back to town and took on the work of finishing the town history. The result is *Lyndon, Gem in the Green*.

    On Dr. Shores's retirement from FSU, a colleague, Marion D. Irish, said, "Venila is an independent soul, with a decent respect for the opinions of others, with courage to speak her own mind. There is no guile or flattery in her, but a sense of humor makes her sometimes salty company." Dr. Shores was called the "Great Stone Face" when she sat in judgment on disciplinary matters—stern, but just and "soft-hearted."

A comment of her "soft-heartedness" appeared in the fall of 1996 issue of the LHS newsletter *Lyndon Legacy*. Patricia (Amidon) Meaden, who grew up in the Lyndonville house that Dr. Shores still owned and maintained, wrote, "Venila had dogs and cats that traveled with her to and from Tallahassee. She had screens installed in the car windows so they could be open when driving through summer heat. Letting this tender side of herself show, especially included remembering her horse Blackie which she had buried with honor behind her Lyndon Center house."

Pat Meaden also wrote, "My parents tried to buy the Lyndonville house but Venila seemed duty-bound to retain her birthplace. We liked to change colors in our ten rooms. Venila saw beauty in only three colors, grey, brown and brownish-grey. Seldom did she really compliment changes we made—her comment was invariably, 'Well, you're the ones who have to live with it!'" Patricia noted that grey with green trim was the color of both Venila's Lyndonville and Lyndon Center houses. Patricia had several pets—a dog, three birds, a rabbit and a white hen. Venila remarked only on the beauty of the cockatiel, "probably because of his deep grey feathers," wrote Pat.

I personally remember that when I was working in the Lyndonville electric office, I used to see Dr. Shores and her mother Alla Shores, usually in the Lyndonville Bank or the Lyndonville electric office when they were at home in Lyndon Center for the summer. They were tall and dignified—and rather imposing figures, at least to my young eyes. Later, when I worked with Miss Shores, as she liked to be called, on our bicentennial committees in the 1970s, I found her a delightful friend and ally, particularly in our efforts to start the Lyndon Historical Society, of which she was a strong supporter. Sometimes LHS or the executive board met in the parlor at her home. She kept coffee hot and ready to serve in a large thermos and prepared refreshments for the meetings.

THE LATE VICTORIAN "WORKING MAN'S HOUSE"

James Shores had a reputation as master carpenter, and many Queen Anne qualities of the late nineteenth century can be seen in the exterior features of the Shores's Lyndon Center house. This handsome but unpretentious home is a fine example of a working man's home. One interior feature is a concave side wall downstairs and a similar feature in the master bedroom upstairs. The dining room hardwood floor is laid with a square piece starting in the center, with the flooring around it laid in much the same manner as a quilter would lay out a "Log Cabin" pattern.

When Dr. Shores died, in 1980, she left the house to the town for a museum, to be known as the Shores Memorial Museum, and left the contents as the Gage Collection, in memory of her parents. In March 1982, the *Caledonian-Record* reported, "A set of house keys and a check for $62,000 were passed across a conference table at the town clerk's office." She left the money for maintenance, but when it came to major repairs, such as a roof, a separate fund called Friends of the Museum was created.

Through the years, much activity went on in the Shores Memorial Museum; one example is an open house held to commemorate the hundredth anniversary of the house on September 21, 1996. It coincided with Lyndon's Fall Foliage Day, and some lucky participants won museum benefit items—a quilt handmade especially for the occasion, as well as pillows, Linda Toborgs's beautiful handmade neckties and maple syrup.

Other projects at the museum included cataloguing, the storing of certain items in archival boxes, painting, papering (paper matching as near as possible to original), building a new shed and holding special exhibits in one of the rooms. Some work was done under the expertise of official museum consultants. For many years, the museum was open to the public for two hours on Saturdays and Sundays, and by appointment for group visits. Some

Dr. Shores's home, deeded to the town of Lyndon for a museum.

LHS meetings were held there, and special exhibits and other activities kept volunteers busy, under the direction of Ruth Hopkins McCarty, who was curator for fifteen years until her retirement.

In 2001, a Shores Memorial Museum steering committing worked on ways to reactivate the museum after needed repair work was completed. The current fundraising campaign was for restoration work on four Lyndon landmarks—the Shores Memorial Museum, the 1809 Town House, the old Lyndon Center school beside the Town House and the Randall covered bridge just off Route 114.

THE VERMONT HOOKED RUG INDUSTRY

The story of rug hooking in town begins with Martha Ross Titcomb, who started the Vermont Hooked Rug Industry at Lyndon Center in 1912. She was born on July 16, 1862, the daughter of Jonathan Ross, chief justice of the Vermont Supreme Court and a former United States senator. The hooked rug business was a boon to farm women, who enjoyed doing something creative during long winter hours. As a "cottage industry," it was also a way for women in rural areas to earn some "pin" money.

Mrs. Titcomb traveled to New Hampshire to consult with a Mrs. Albee, who had started her own rug-hooking business. It did not require expensive equipment or materials, and Martha, being an artist, could provide designs and marketing know-how for the ladies at Lyndon Center. They started with wool strips from old garments and other woolen goods. Then Martha met a Mr. Huick from a wool-spinning mill in Albany, New York. Wool from this mill came in rich, vibrant colors done with German dyes.

Martha sent examples of work by the industrious rug hookers to Detroit and Chicago to be sold through Women's Exchanges. It was said that Martha got the thrill of her life with the first order. It came from a Chicago interior decorator, Elsie DeWolfe. Other decorators began to hear of these talented Vermont women and sent orders, sometimes for rugs as large as nine by twelve feet. Neighbors would help by piecing together sections for large rugs.

Elizabeth Titcomb Connor died in Shelburne on October 17, 2000, at 101 years of age. Her obituary appeared in the *Caledonian-Record*. She was a 1917 graduate of Lyndon Institute, and after graduating from Bryn Mawr College in Pennsylvania and the Fontainebleau School in Paris, she worked for a while with her mother in the Vermont Hooked Rug Industry. When Martha Titcomb died just before World War II, the rug-hooking industry at Lyndon Center faded away.

Elizabeth Titcomb Connor, ninety-eight years of age, came to her eightieth reunion at Lyndon Institute in 1997. Alumni president, Dwight Davis, presents her with plaque in commemoration.

Liz Connor opened a Swap Shop in Woodstock in 1939, which she ran for several years, and then she started Glad Rags sales to benefit the Vermont Children's Aid Society. When she closed her house in Woodstock at age ninety, she found a forgotten, partial hooked rug designed by her mother, Martha Titcomb, and she also found all the wool dyed to complete it. A volunteer completed the floral-designed rug. It is the last piece of Martha Titcomb's work and a historic reminder of the Vermont Hooked Rug Industry.

In 1990, as part of the plans for the upcoming Lyndon town bicentennial, celebrated in 1991, ideas included looking into the history of some old cottage industries of this town. A group of women interested in rug hooking met at the Senior Center on Church Street. An information meeting was held soon after at Lyndon Institute, and the rug hookers were off and running. Diane (Squires) Lentine, with roots in Lyndon Center, had been hooking rugs in Connecticut since 1986, and had already caught the interest of some of her relatives here in town in this creative craft (Leone Hopkins Gale and Eleanor Hopkins Wright, for instance).

The Lyn-Burke Wooly Hookers was a large, enthusiastic group within the Green Mountain Rug Hookers Guild. The Woolys met for some time during the summer for the Thursday "Hook-in" at Diane Lentine's home

A Glance Back in Time

Rug-hooking session at Diane Lentine's home on Vail Hill. *From left:* AnnLouise Smith, Anita Zentz, Diane Lentine, Beverly Delnicki, Leone Gale and Barbara Bessette, 2000.

(the former Squires's house) on Vail Hill. Each member worked on her own project, be it a rug, small or large, a wall hanging or chair seats. The idea of working in groups is fun as well as an opportunity to exchange ideas and helpful suggestions. Books on rug hooking in memory of Ruth Haslam are available at the Cobleigh Library. Some of the Wooly Hookers attend workshops where they can browse through many designs, books and materials and meet people from other countries with different ideas for designs.

The Complete Book of Rug Hooking, by Joan Moshimer, tells how women used to draw directly onto an old feed sack with a piece of charcoal. "Naive charm, strange looking animals, was the result of this freehand attempt to portray barnyard creatures or pets." Designs from kitchen plates were another way of producing drawings for hooking. The early rug hookers were using means of expressing their own personalities in their original creations. The women made dyes from many flowers, plants and shrubs for yellows, greens, reds, blues and browns.

Moshimer tells of sailors who frequently hooked rugs on long sea journeys, using canvas for foundation and yarns or short strands from rope. Their designs often resembled full-rigged ships, anchors and whales.

By the middle of the 1800s, Edward Sands Frost of Biddeford, Maine, made stencils of tin, selling them from his peddler's wagon to housewives along his route. Being a machinist he devised a crooked hook when he noticed his wife using a poorly made hook. He made designs on paper and got orders for patterns. He became known as "the rug man," but some felt that the ready-made patterns stifled the creativity of housewives.

About the same time, a dyer from a small woolen mill in Foxcroft, Maine, developed dyes for home use to replace the time-consuming work of vegetable dyeing. This became the well-known Cushing Company, now owned by Craftsman Studio in Kennebunkport. Many of today's rug hookers are still consumers of Cushing dyes.

Charlotte K. Stratton bought tons of Frost stencils to use in her business, but eventually sold them to the Henry Ford Museum in Dearborn, Michigan. At the museum, hooking bees are being done similar to those in the nineteenth century in order to preserve the old methods.

In the meantime, the former Lyn-Burke Wooly Hookers (spread out in other groups now) are still preserving this long-ago craft, once doomed because of the machine age, but now making a lively comeback with beautiful results. The results not only win prizes at fairs and other competitions, but also produce beautiful rugs and other creations that would no doubt give much pleasure to Martha Titcomb and her daughter Elizabeth Connor if they could see them.

THE VICTORY CORPS SKI TEAM

In the December 2003 *North Star*, Doug Conly wrote about the induction of veterans Delmas Devenger and others from the Tenth Mountain Division of World War II into the Vermont Ski Hall of Fame. In the November 8, 2003 *Caledonian-Record*, Isaac Olson wrote about Edward Meilleur of St. Johnsbury and Donald Erskine of Lyndonville, who were with the Tenth Mountain Division and were also inducted (Erskine posthumously) into the Vermont Ski Hall of Fame.

This all brought to mind the Victory Corps Ski Team at Lyndon Institute in the 1940s. When I was researching files at Lyndon Institute for the sports chapter of the *Images of America, Lyndon Institute* book, I was looking through many pictures with Merlyn Courser, the then athletic director. The photo labeled "Lyndon Institute Victory Corps Ski Team" intrigued us and we wondered what was this "Victory Corps Ski Team." The year 1943 was much earlier than Merlyn's high school days and much later than mine. The answer was in the 1943 student yearbook, the *Cynosure*.

In 1943, the United States Army requested that high schools initiate a Victory Corps program. The objective throughout the country was to condition students for national service. An hour and a half on every Tuesday afternoon was devoted to Victory Corps programs. For the girls, it included hygiene, first aid, child welfare, French interpretation and office practice. For the boys, it was organized training in skating and skiing. The *Cynosure* stated, "Under the supervision of Mr. R.K. Lewis, history teacher and coach, and with assistance of the Vermont State Guard, preliminary military training was designed to accustom future enlisted men to the fundamentals of army discipline."

The sudden importance of technical arts gave both boys and girls alike the opportunity to receive instruction in blueprint reading and mechanical

Skiing For Victory. *From left:* George Guy, Howard Garfield, Norman Lavely, Doug Thompson, Elmer Brown, Dick Wheeler, Edgar Kellaway, Norman Leach, Raymond Mathers, Eddie Smith, Delmar Leach, Wayne Brown, Howard Wakefield, Duane Pierce and Franz Smith. *Courtesy of Lyndon Institute.*

drawing. Perhaps the boys' cooking class had nothing to do with the war, but many boys asked for such a class. The *Cynosure* said, "Now every Friday afternoon we smell in the corridors and basements the surprisingly fragrant aroma of apple pies (sometimes burnt a bit, of course), cookies and griddle cakes."

Other Victory Corps courses at LI listed for the 1943–44 year included surgical dressing for girls, thirty-one of whom volunteered to make Red Cross dressings. Military drill for boys included military courtesy and discipline, with their importance to civilian life. Students worked to increase the sales of war stamps and bonds in the school. Other courses included learning fundamentals of radio, aeronautics, military drill for boys and skiing and skating patrol for girls.

A member of the Lyndon Institute Victory Corps Ski Team, Wayne Brown remembers that one afternoon a week, the team would go to fields and hills—not where there were rope tows and lifts—and practice what would have been maneuvers similar to those practiced by the U.S. Army Mountain Troops, who trained in Fort Hale, Colorado.

In the meantime, LI skiers, with some help from older members, also kept Lyndon Outing Club (LOC) going when so many people were busy with the war effort. That is why LOC, started in 1936, has the credit of being the only volunteer outdoor recreation club that has never closed since it first began. Many young skiers, including Donald Erskine, acquired their skill learning and practicing on the Oscar Baril farm pasture slopes and on the thirty-five-meter jump (later rebuilt to forty-five meters) in the Fletcher pasture nearby. In 1947, the whole LOC operation moved to the Shonyo farm hills, to what is now known as Shonyo Park. From the beginning, LOC had lights, so practicing wasn't limited to just daylight hours.

The Victory Corps skiers had no team uniform. As the photo shows, they had on the regular clothes they wore to school—sweaters or jackets. Some of them may have been on the regular ski or other sports teams and earned the athletic "L" shown on some of the sweaters. By the time these skiers graduated from Lyndon Institute, the war was almost over, and they never did join the Tenth Mountain Division, although some of them did serve in armed forces.

Donald Erskine wasn't on the LI Victory Corps Ski Team. He was in the real thing, having enlisted in the Tenth Mountain Division in 1942. He was a technical sergeant on the Division Signal Corps radio and ski patrol in the Apennine Valley in Italy until 1946. He came back to LI, graduated in 1947 and attended the University of Vermont in addition to pursuing specialized studies at Norwich University, MIT, Dartmouth College and Massachusetts Radio School.

He was part of the LI faculty, teaching science courses, initiating college courses of study in physics and chemistry and coaching the LI ski team to many victories—thirteen times district champions, nine times state champions and five times New England champions. Later, he was a research engineer at the Lyndonville Vermont American Company (Vermont Tap & Die) and then at Northeast Tool. He died in 1988 at age sixty-three. Lyndonville can be proud of him, of his many accomplishments in technology and science and of his leading the LI ski team to so many victories.

THE OLD MEETINGHOUSE OF 1809

When towns were new and there were no churches or town halls yet built, an itinerant preacher might hold religious services in people's houses. As for town meetings, the first in Lyndon was held on July 4, 1791, in Daniel Reniff's log cabin, on what we know today as Vail Hill Road. A marker by the road commemorates this first town meeting. After that, town meetings were held many times in the Cahoon house on Red Village Road.

The Town House at Lyndon Center is the oldest public building in the town of Lyndon. This is reminder of what this important historical building has meant to townspeople for almost two hundred years and the changes it has undergone as it has been adapted to various uses.

On December 23, 1800, fifty-one men signed a document, becoming members of an organization called "The Religious Society for the Purpose of Promoting Public Preaching of the Gospel in Said Town." A committee was instructed to find a lot for a meetinghouse as near the center of town as could be procured. Job Sheldon came forth with six acres to be used, not only for the meetinghouse, but also for a burying ground and a common parade ground for the hometown militia practice field. The deed to the town also allowed for a road through the property.

When the building was finished in 1809, it served as a place for religious services as well as a hall for town meetings. Four denominations mainly shared the building—Congregationalists, Baptists, Methodists and Universalists—each with its own service by turns. Some people attended even when it was not their own denomination holding the service.

Charles M. Chase wrote in the *Vermont Union* that the meetinghouse "was in the church architecture of that day, two stories high, having square box pews. The pews were so high that only the heads of the tallest appeared

The old meetinghouse when it was being used as a town hall.

above the top." That wouldn't leave much opportunity for boys and girls to make eyes at each other across the room.

The pulpit was a large, square box. The gallery also had high box pews on two walls, and there were two rows of benches for the singers. It has been said that there was quite a rivalry among the singers of the various denominations, some of whom sang at every service. The belfry was enclosed and in front, rather than in a steeple on top.

On the one hundredth anniversary, at a 1909 meeting, a paper written by Mrs. Curtis Stevens was read in which she described a service of 1840. Services began at 10:30 a.m. In those days, it would have taken quite some time for those not living near to prepare a lunch to carry, dress appropriately, fill foot stoves with coals, harness the horses and drive to the meetinghouse at Lyndon Center.

It would also have taken time for someone to get the two wood stoves in the meetinghouse stoked to warm up the hall. Stove pipes running the length of the room and across the end would help with warmth. Those coming from a distance brought in their own foot stoves that had kept their feet warm in their sleighs. Sheds provided shelter for the horses. Though the meetinghouse stoves gave off a good amount of heat, floors far away from the stoves were usually quite cold. The foot stoves could be reheated at noon with coals from the Town House stoves for the afternoon service and the long drive home afterward.

A Glance Back in Time

Mrs. Stevens had the foresight to describe the style of clothing worn to meeting in 1840, and we can better picture the scene of long ago. She wrote,

> *The Graves girls dressed alike. They had quilted hoods of green worsted goods faced with pink silk. In summer they wore poke bonnets faced with artificial flowers, most becoming to the red cheeks and bright eyes of the fair country girls. These were the days of full skirts, big sleeves, hand embroidered lace collars and undersleeves, mitts, long fingerless gloves in summer and mittens in winter. The men took pride in their high neck stocks, coat collars, swallowtails and stove pipe hats.*

The sermon was of "goodly length extending to the 7thlies and 8thlies," Mrs. Curtis said. When the morning closed, the town clerk stepped forward from his pew and announced the marriage intentions. There was also time for relating personal experiences. Sunday school followed this, and then time for lunch, which many brought due to traveling long distances. The afternoon service, an hour and a half long, was similar to the morning service, with scripture, hymns and a sermon.

About 1850, most church societies had built churches of their own in other sections of town. Some of the pews were removed, but the town had to pay a dollar to each pew owner to continue town meetings there. By 1860, major changes had altered the appearance of the old meetinghouse. The enclosed belfry on the front had been taken off and the space left was boarded and clapboarded to become part of the straight front. A seven-foot-wide piazza was added across the front.

The old Town House (as it came to be called) saw many other uses besides town meetings after the church societies left. In 1945, a hardwood floor was laid, which made a good dance floor, with musicians on stage—one group was Don Fields and the Pony Boys. For a while, the Town House was adapted for theater use by the Carriage Wheel Playhouse. The Town House was newly painted in 1991 in preparation for the Lyndon Bicentennial.

Town meetings continued here until large attendance made the space inadequate. From 1971, town meetings were held in the Lyndon Institute auditorium and voting for elections was held in the municipal building, the former Lyndonville Graded School. Now town meetings and voting take place in the Lyndon Town School, built in 1991.

Seats in the Town House are historical as well. They are connected seats from the old Music Hall. The object of having connected seats in the Music Hall was so they could be pushed back under the balcony, a whole row at a time, to make room for dancing or other open-space entertainment such as festivals and, in later years, donkey basketball and roller skating.

Some photos of the former meetinghouse may say "Town Hall" on the front. Since it is no longer used for town meetings, town historian Dr. Venila Shores suggested that it would be more appropriate to change the name to its historical designation—"Town House"—a better reminder that its main purpose for so many year was as a religious meetinghouse and a town hall. Though the Town House, the Shores Memorial and the District Six School are owned by the Town of Lyndon, they are under the direction of the Lyndon Historical Society. LHS and Lyndon Institute have a partnership, agreed to by the town, that LI will use these facilities for many of their studies and workshops.

THE SLEEPING BABE MONUMENT, EMBLEM OF ETERNAL REST

A lot of people ask about the Sleeping Babe monument at the Lyndon Center cemetery—what it means, who did it and the sayings inscribed on it. A number of years ago, it was written up and a short version and a photo of it appear in a booklet, *Look Around Lyndon*, printed in 1978. For those who are looking for more information and the complete quotes, I offer this account of the Sleeping Babe of Eternal Rest.

Every Memorial Day for many years, through gun salutes and the strains of funereal music played by the Lyndonville Military Band and the haunting sound of "Taps," the beautiful babe sleeps peacefully through another ceremony. "A Dreamless Sleep, Emblem of Eternal Rest" were the words cut on the marble monument many years ago.

The stone itself is a simple block, but made impressive with its columns, one on each corner and the sleeping babe on a smaller block on top, his head resting in his hands on a pillow. A rosebud, a symbol of a life unfolded, lies at the child's back.

Stonecutter Gratis P. Spencer worked on the ambitious monument for years at his home in Lyndon, where he plied his trade. He erected it sometime before his own death in 1908. Headstones of four of his children who died in childhood are in the lot with the Sleeping Babe tombstone. A most skillful workman and well known in a large surrounding area, Mr. Spencer cut many beautiful monuments and tombstones.

His advertisements stated that "at Spencer's Marble Works at Lyndon, Vt., can be found a good assortment of monumental gravestones and tablets manufactured from foreign and domestic marble of all kinds and shades of color to suit everybody in price and variety of style."

Gratis P. Spencer was born in Bloomfield, March 7, 1825, the son of Gratis P. and Susan Dearth Spencer. He came to Lyndon sometime in the

The Sleeping Babe monument, work of stonecutter Gratis P. Spencer.

1850s. He married Annette Caswell of Lisbon, New Hampshire. When G.P. Spencer died on January 15, 1908, less than two months before his eighty-third birthday, he had been confined to his bed only a few days.

   In September 1905, he had taken, for the last time, his usual walk from his place, where he lived on the back Lyndon Center road down to Lyndon Corner. He enjoyed remarkably good health for a while after that. He was survived by five children: Fred, Frank and George of Lyndon; William of Waterbury; and Lulu Spencer Lawrence of Waltham, Massachusetts. G.P. Spencer was unusually kindhearted, said his obituary, and an indulgent husband and father. He was a great reader and possessed much interesting information.

Many people called Spencer an atheist, but some more kindly disposed termed him a naturalist. Perhaps the death of four of his nine children at an early age made him bitter. Passed down through local history is the legend that some considered the quotes on his stone blasphemous and tried to obliterate them. Whether this is true or not, one side of the monument is blank and the other sides have certainly deteriorated with weather and time (marble does not stand up as well as granite).

Since he can no longer speak for himself, people form their own opinions as they read what they can of the curious ranting. Luckily, the inscriptions were written down as best as could be read many years before they became really worn. To the best of my knowledge, as well as that of Dr. Venila Shores, former official town historian, they are:

> *Natural law is of universal application and all truth is manifest to sense. Of all deceivers who have plagued mankind none are so dearly ruinous to human happiness as those imposters who pretend to lead men by a light above nature.*

On another side:

> *The lips of the dead are closed forever. There comes no voice from the tomb. Christianity is responsible for having cast the glare of eternal fire onto almost every grave. All stories of gods & devils, of heavens and hells, as they do not conform to nature & are not apparent to sense should be rejected without consideration.*
>
> *Science has never killed or persecuted a single person for doubting or deny its teachings, and most of these teachings have been true, but religion has murdered millions for doubting or denying dogmas and most of these dogmas have been false.*
>
> *Beyond the universe there is nothing; and within the universe the supernatural does not exist.*
>
> *Man will go down into the grave and all his thoughts will perish. The uneasy consciousness which is his remote corner of the universe will be at rest. Matter will know it all no longer. Imperishable monuments and immortal deeds, death itself and love stronger than death will be as though they had never been. Nor will anything that is, be better or be worse for all that labor, genius, devotion and suffering of man have striven through countless ages to effect.*

When the photo on page 120 was taken in 1978, the monument was in good condition. In the thirty years since, it has deteriorated to the extent that there are broken columns and corners. It would take a lot of money to restore it to its original beauty.

Whether one does or does not believe in Spencer's writings is not important. What *is* important is the significance of the beautiful monument itself and the historical and artistic heritage of the stonecutter Gratis P. Spencer. It has become a Lyndon landmark.

CAMP VAIL AND SOLDIERS OF THE SOIL

Do echoes of a hoe striking a stone or a cutter bar mowing hay still linger over Vail Hill? Is there a scent of newly mown hay or freshly cut corn in the air? Residential Speedwell Estates, with its streets and homes, was once known as Speedwell Farms and hummed with activity in fields and barns. When it was all part of the state agricultural school, even echoes of World War I reached these Vermont Hills.

In 1918, when older sons were "over there" fighting in World War I, younger sons were "over here" heeding the call to Camp Vail at Lyndon Center.

> As never in her history <u>Vermont</u> must use her hills this summer. The <u>World</u> is calling for food. The <u>Soldier Sons of Vermont</u> have gone to fight the world's battle. <u>Vermont</u> cannot, must not desert them. The hills and fields of <u>Old Vermont Must</u> bring forth their treasures to <u>Back Them Up</u>. <u>Younger Sons—You've Got to Help</u>.
>
> The farmers need hundreds of hands to care for and harvest crops. They want the service of strong red blooded boys from 16 to 20 years of age. They are willing to pay good wages. The <u>State of Vermont</u> through the Department of Agriculture proposes to <u>Enlist Her Boys for the Farm</u>. At the Theodore N. Vail School of Agriculture and Farms, <u>Camp Vail</u> is to be established. The purpose is to recruit, select and train boys for farm work.

It was noted that farm boys were already engaged in farming at home, but boys (as male youths were called in those days) from large towns and cities needed farm training.

The four purposes stated were: "To start the boys in the ways and hours of the farm; to give them some opportunity to harden their muscles for the summer's work; to teach them some of the simple farming operations; and to instill within them a real desire to serve their country in the production of food."

There were three camps of two weeks each—starting May 20, June 3 and June 17—with a maximum of fifty boys in each camp. They were divided into squads of ten each and were under charge of a supervisor/instructor. After training, the boys were to be sent to "Carefully selected Vermont Farms" to work for just and fair wages, or were sent back home in reserve until needed. All expenses were paid by the state except carfare to the camp. Each boy had to agree to give to Vermont a summer of his best service on a Vermont farm.

It was 1910 when Theodore N. Vail, president of the American Telephone and Telegraph Company, had established the agricultural school on his Speedwell Farms estate. It became the Lyndon School of Agriculture. Tuition was free—the agricultural school was supported by Mr. Vail's private funds. While the farm school and Lyndon Institute were two separate institutions, both cooperated in the use of facilities and some teachers.

In 1915, Vail made a gift of the agricultural school and farms to the State of Vermont. The passage by legislature of Act No. Sixteen gave approval on March 31, 1915, for the Theodore N. Vail Agricultural School and Farms, which became an important part of the state system of public education. When the State of Vermont gave up the agricultural school in 1922, it reverted to Lyndon Institute.

In 1918, the agricultural school, still state owned, was an ideal setup for the training of boys to "produce food to aid the war effort instead of wasting a summer." The appeal for Camp Vail was made all over the state. Under skilled supervisors, boys were selected, "weeding" out those physically incompetent or those whose "laziness" would render them "useless" on a farm. The director of the T.N. Vail Agricultural School, Rollo Reynolds, was appointed director of Camp Vail. There was also a military commandant, a camp physician, camp dentist, seven agricultural supervisors and a camp steward.

A 1918 *Vermonter* magazine article gave an account and photos of Camp Vail activities. The bugler's "first call" sounded at daybreak. "From the tents of white lining the company street tumble forth lads—just lads—with tousled heads and sleep still in their eyes." The flag was raised and the lads dashed across the drill ground to the washroom.

After the flag raising, fifteen minutes of exercises took place on the drill ground (the Lyndon Institute campus), followed by tent inspection and then mess. The five squads were then given the orders of the day: Squad One, dairying and horses; Squad Two, haying machinery and main farm; Squad Three, forage crops and potatoes; Squad Four, wood cutting; and Squad

A Glance Back in Time

CAMP VAIL.

Soldiers of the Soil stand at attention (at top) during the 5:30 a.m. reveille—every morning! *Courtesy of the 1915 T.N. Vail Agricultural School and Farms of Vermont catalog.*

The "soldiers" learn how to work the soil.

Five, truck gardening. Right face! Forward march! And all fell in to their assorted tasks.

Camp supervisors taking squad leadership roles included Harley Leland, Carroll Pike, Jerome Fitzpatrick, George Blood and Harold Billings. Others involved were Seth T. Wheat and George Burnham. Harvey Wingate was the commandant and Rollo G. Reynolds the director.

The school farm was on the hill above the Lyndon Institute campus, and here the boys learned to feed and milk cows. In the creamery, they washed pails and cans and separated the milk. Those assigned to horses for the day learned how to harness and unharness, operate the mowing machine and the horse rake and how to repair any machine sections that might break. Some were assigned to haying. There was plowing, harrowing, planting, hoeing and woodcutting. The crosscut saw could prove a boy's ability to "keep up his end." At the truck garden that supplied the school, the boys became familiar with hoe, hand and horse cultivators, horse hoe and the horse planter. Squad assignments were changed from day to day so all could learn everything. Camp Vail boys were not required to take academic courses as were required of the regular agricultural school year students.

The squads marched back to the campus at 11:30 a.m. for dinner (a farmer's good, square meal), which disappeared "as if by magic." Afternoon orders included an hour and a half of military drills for training in obedience and teamwork. At 4:00 p.m., all returned to the campus, where a bugle sounded the lowering of the colors. After showers and mess, there was time for baseball, football, tennis and track. Evening activities might include a company drill, a camp sing or a noted speaker. Several times, the boys were taken to "town" for meetings having to do with the war. One night a week, they were given "leave" to go to Lyndonville. They were encouraged to attend a church on Sundays. Sunday afternoon was free for letter writing—Camp Vail stationery was provided. The dormitory reading room was supplied with farm papers, periodicals, newspapers and books.

Camp Vail was the impartial judge as to the treatment of a boy placed on a farm, or as to the farmer's satisfaction or dissatisfaction with the boy. If one proved unsatisfactory, the director would remove him and send the farmer another.

Some of the boys found that through physical hard work they had more stamina and perseverance than they realized. It was believed that the work in potato fields under the hot sun would demonstrate this as much as any of the other work.

"It is 9 p.m.," says the *Vermonter.* "The shadows have fallen over the camp." With the sound of "Taps," the lights on the company street go out. "The camp is quiet" and fifty "Soldiers of the Soil, The Hope of Tomorrow's World," are asleep.

THE NEWS IN LYNDON

Until 1865, residents had to depend on newspapers from other locations, or go without. Some did get the *Caledonian*, which began as a weekly in 1837, or the *North Star*, a weekly published in Danville. Then, in 1865, a newspaper was published in Lyndon (Corner). Volume one, number one of the *Vermont Union* came out on February 10, 1865.

Charles M. Chase, music teacher, choir director, newspaper editor, correspondent, lawyer, police magistrate and many other things he had been in the Midwest, came back home to Lyndon for a visit in 1864. His father, Epaphras B. Chase was not well by then, and Charles stayed on. His experience with newspapers in Illinois no doubt made him realize that Lyndon could use its own newspaper. He purchased a newspaper plant in Newport and moved it to the Dana Block at Lyndon Corner.

In those days, newspapers covered local news, but it was inside the paper. On page one of Chase's first *Union*, the masthead stated that the paper was $2.50 per annum. There was a Civil War poem, a story called "The Lace Maker" and little stories and items, but no news. Page two carried news from around the country, the Civil War and General Sherman's Letter. One item says "Gold closed at $2.05."

Page three gets a little more local, with "Local Intelligence," giving news around the area; one item thanks Sheffield for fifty-four subscriptions. Local ads, mostly from Lyndon, but including some from St. Johnsbury and a few others, covered a large part of page three. Page four was given over entirely to agricultural news and reports.

It wasn't long before Chase gave localities within the scope of the paper's circulation their own heading by town or locality name, and it was the first newspaper in the United States to do this. This gave villages and towns, in a sense, the feeling that they had a "home-town" newspaper.

Charles M. Chase, the dedicated newsman.

A Glance Back in Time

Wow! That's news!

Charles M. Chase made annual trips to distant states, and due to his correspondence for publication in his paper, the *Union* acquired more than a local reputation. Between 1870 and 1890, the *Union* reached a circulation of three thousand, which seemed remarkable in later years to Charles's son, John Bryant Chase, because it was published in a town of such small size.

Much of Charles's writing shows the great sense of humor he possessed. He still loved music, and composed and published numerous church hymns as well as "The Vermont Union Polka," "Girl Baby Polka" and "The Vermont Union Waltz."

The *Vermont Union* suffered no gap in its production when Charles M. Chase died on November 1, 1902, a few days before his seventy-third birthday. Charles's son John had returned to Lyndon from his work on the *Bradford Opinion* in Bradford, Vermont, and had taken over the paper during his father's illness. Some of John's newspaper experience was acquired when he worked in his father's paper after school when he was twelve to fourteen years old. There were no folding machines then and he had to fold 2,500 to 3,000 newspapers by hand. "It was lively but not hard work and we used to have a good time seeing who could fold the fastest," he wrote many years later. When he was high school age, he learned compositing and typesetting. He was also encouraged to do some local reporting, his "stories usually being accepted after the blue penciling they merited."

In the meantime, in 1899, a new weekly newspaper started in Lyndonville. It was the *Lyndonville Journal*, issued by H.B. Davis, who for thirty years had been foreman of the St. Johnsbury *Caledonian* plant. A succession of owners of the *Lyndonville Journal* included Allen S. Holbrook and J. Harold Fuller; for a long time, B.U. Wells was the publisher. John Chase acquired the *Lyndonville Journal*, merged it with the *Vermont Union* and on November 1,

1905, his publication became the *Vermont Union-Journal* and stayed in the Dodge and Watson Block at the west-end room.

John wrote with a sense of history, often copying some of his father's writing and adding his own comments on special occasions, such as anniversaries of events. John also wrote biographies of families in the area. His well-known, much-anticipated and often clipped-and-saved column was called "Rambling Paragraphs." John seemed to be of a more serious nature than his father, but newspaper styles had changed and the personal, humorous situations that often appeared in the earlier papers of his father were no longer as appropriate.

John B. Chase married Elisabeth Jones from Bradford. She operated the maple candy business from their home (now Cupola Apartments). John was a community and civic worker, and was often in demand as a speaker. He retired in 1941, selling the *Union* to the *Caledonian-Record*. He died on November 21, 1960.

These old newspapers are great leads to history. It is known that mistakes may have been made, but local newspaper items can be checked with official records, and almost always have many more interesting details. In some cases, the newspapers are almost the only source for local history.

The *Lyndonville Journal*, dated July 1, 1896, is a special illustrated edition of "Lyndonville, the Hustling Railroad Village," with sketches and illustrations of its leading industries, buildings and citizens. It is considered an invaluable historical treasure-trove.

THE OLDEST CHURCH IN TOWN

The bell of the First Congregational Church on York Street at Lyndon Corner will ring Sunday evening, August 24, 1997, for a 7 o'clock service. The Reverend Donald Vincent, pastor of the First Congregational Church of Lyndonville will be the minister for this yearly occasion." This is the oldest church in the town of Lyndon and has a long history. It was organized by nine people 180 years ago, on November 30, 1817.

Until the church itself was built, the congregation met in various homes. The Reverend Samuel G. Tenney was ordained and installed on June 22, 1825, with a salary of $400 per year. The church building, begun in 1827, was dedicated and occupied in January 1829. It cost $4,000 and seated 300 people. One printed roll lists all 414 members of the church between 1817 and 1892.

When Reverend William Scales began preaching in 1836, the pay was $400 per year, "one-half in good merchantable grain." In 1855, the pay was $600 per year "and perhaps a donation." In 1867, it was $800 per year "and a house to live in."

Church societies included the Ladies' Home Missionary; the Woman's Board of Foreign Missions; Young People's Missionary Society; Children's Missionary Society; and Christian Endeavor, a young people's group. In 1861, the Ladies Sewing Circle was making clothes for the Third Vermont Regiment in the Civil War.

The church observed its centennial on August 15, 1917. Arthur F. Stone of St. Johnsbury, the grandson of an early deacon, Charles Stone, gave an address entitled, "Faith of Our Fathers." As an older resident, Mabel Hall Walter (Mrs. Charles T. Walter) was asked to prepare reminiscences.

Mrs. Walter told about the pipe organ that was built for the old North Church of St. Johnsbury and bought for the Lyndon church in 1846 for $300.

The Lyndon Congregational Church, circa 1899.

It was in the high gallery at the back of the Lyndon church. The congregation stood and faced the choir in the gallery when hymns were sung.

The organ became temperamental and only Charles M. Chase, musician and publisher of the *Vermont Union*, "understood its whims and could draw noble strains from it." After he was gone, others tried, but sometimes keys stuck and there would be squeals. Then the choir would run to the cabinet organ, an 1872 purchase, and continue singing. When the gallery was torn down in 1881, the pipe organ was moved down to the platform. The front section was taken out and the cabinet organ set in front of it, making it appear to be a pipe organ, where it stands today.

A Glance Back in Time

The organ pipes came from the original 1846 organ.

The chancel of the historic church.

A Glance Back in Time

The brass chandelier had dangling glass prisms. "It was a gorgeous sight when lighted," Mrs. Walter said. The prisms were later removed, perhaps because they were distracting when summer breezes from the open windows sent them to "tinkling musically." Years later, the brass chandelier was wired for electricity. Mrs. Walter also remembered two handsome colored china vases with bouquets of flowers. She recalled the robin's-egg-blue bookmark in the pulpit Bible. It hung from the Bible in three tiers, each one with a different cross, the beautiful handwork of Grandma Goss and her sister, Mrs. Swan.

Sometimes there were startling moments. When the church was remodeled in 1854, the pulpit was reached by three steep steps up from the platform. Reverend E.T. Fairbanks, then a young minister, was preaching in exchange. He startled the congregation when he fell down these steep steps as he descended from the pulpit. Another startling moment was the time when one good deacon, after a pinch of snuff, sneezed so violently that he ejected his false teeth across the aisle. Once a pigeon flew from the belfry and through a high, small window opened for ventilation. The pigeon landed on Reverend Wells's head during prayer. Without missing a word or opening his eyes, he reached up and startled the pigeon, which flew around the room, but again perched on Reverend Wells's head and stayed until the prayer was finished. It was awe-inspiring and made the congregation think of John the Baptist when the "spirit of the dove descended upon him."

The thriving village of Lyndon changed to a quiet place of residence after the hotel and some stores were destroyed by fire, and after the Lyndon Carriage Company and the Lyndon Mill Company closed—all places of employment. The bank, doctors' and lawyers' offices, hardware store and others closed or moved to Lyndonville, which was flourishing because of the railroad.

Though it has been a number of years or more since regular services were given up at the Lyndon church, a yearly service keeps its charter. Occasionally, a wedding or other event takes place there. Some remember a few years ago when the pews were draped with quilts for an impressive quilt show.

The brass chandelier, though now powered by electricity, the ancient organ pipes behind the old cabinet organ, the pews and the wide floorboards are some of the old-time features that give the church its reverential historic stamp. The bell in the steeple was made in Boston by Henry N. Cooper in 1855. Eric Chester, one of several who for a long time kept tabs on the church, gave the rope a pull once in a while just to make sure the bell could still ring. The few remaining members hope this old historic church can be preserved, even if used for other purposes, if there was some way the funds for restoration could be found.

THE ACADEMIES IN LYNDON

The stark, empty walls standing on South Wheelock Road at Lyndon Corner are a reminder of a proud school as it once was—the Lyndon Academy and Graded School—until devastated by fire on November 19, 2002. Part of the building was rebuilt in 2004 and is no longer stark and empty—it is now Steele's Antiques & Emporium. Another vestige of the old school is its bell, now in its third location. Not in a belfry this time, it is preserved and displayed as an artifact at the Lyndon Town School.

Lyndon actually had two academies. The first was the County Grammar School at Lyndon, which was chartered on November 12, 1831, and opened for its first session in the fall of 1832. Later it was renamed Lyndon Academy. You can see it today as an apartment house located on a rise of land that sets it higher than the other buildings on Chapel Street, Route 5, at Lyndon Corner.

Although intended to be secondary schools, grammar schools in the early days were not like the secondary schools of today. Requirements read, "All inhabitants of the county of Caledonia shall be admitted as pupils who are so far advanced as to be able to be capable of reading a sentence intelligibly so as to study English grammar to advantage." Supposedly this "requirement" was acquired in the "common schools." No pupils under the age of eight were to be admitted in the grammar school.

Lyndon Academy students wended their way up the steps of several terraces, five steps to each terrace, leading up to the front door. The bell, then in the belfry atop the building, was rung by pulling a rope hung from a closet off the front hall. The teacher's desk was on a raised platform in the schoolroom, facing four rows of benches, five seats to a row. Philosophy, chemistry and astronomy were taught on the second floor. In my own family collection of artifacts is an old astronomy book, in which my great-aunt Abigail Fletcher signed her name.

The old Lyndon Grammar School (Lyndon Academy in its later days). *Courtesy of James Herrity.*

A committee of trustees petitioned the Vermont General Assembly for funds from the county grammar school lease lands for Lyndon. The law passed, but Peacham Academy, chartered much earlier as the County Grammar School in 1795, claimed that it was entitled to all the fees from the county grammar school lands.

Years of legal charges and countercharges followed, with some of the best lawyers of the state representing both schools, but finally Judge Collamer of the Vermont Supreme Court agreed that Peacham Academy should not be deprived of its lease lands. Lease land tenants of Lyndon, St. Johnsbury, Burke, Kirby and Sheffield were required to continue paying rent to the County Grammar School (Peacham Academy, as it came to be more familiarly known). During the nineteen years that my husband and our family resided in the Mount Hunger area of Lyndon, and had a deed, we paid land rent, about thirty-five cents a year, to Peacham Academy.

Not getting the funds from the grammar school lands for Lyndon Academy made for financial difficulties, but with private funds the Lyndon Academy flourished for a good thirty-five years, at times with as many as one hundred students. Tuition was three dollars per term, and three dollars and sixty cents if mathematics, language and drawing were included. Preceptors were college graduates as well as religious men who could fill a pulpit.

Dorothy Walter, who lived out her retired life at her childhood home, Riverside, supplied information on the "Corner" schools a long time ago. She said that some of the "professors" of the early Lyndon Academy were often new college graduates, "who after winning their spurs ruling over boys and girls for a time, and often courting and marrying some pretty local young lady, went on to long service as teachers in bigger places or schools."

Unable to keep going, Lyndon Academy closed in 1866 or 1867, and it was sold at auction to C.M. Chase for $500 and made into a boardinghouse for a time. When H.H. Streeter bought it, he ran it as Woodlawn Hotel until 1880, when it sold to different private owners over the subsequent years.

In 1872, a new two-story school was built on the road that leads to South Wheelock and dedicated on February 23, 1872, as the Lyndon Academy and Graded School. It took the place of four schools: the old Lyndon Academy and three one-room schools in the Lyndon Corner area (Ledge School, Trefren School and Cahoon School). The catalogue for the new Lyndon Academy and Graded School read, "Lyndon is delightfully situated in the Passumpsic valley on the Boston and Maine R.R. The school, commodious and convenient, is within five minutes walk from the R. Station." That would be the Lyndon station, located near where the Gulf Service station stands today.

The Lyndon Academy and Graded School, built in 1872, eventually became the graded school for Lyndon Corner pupils.

Gathered at the front entrance of the Lyndon Academy and Graded School, all unidentified today.

Also printed in the catalog: "All students were required to take Rhetoricals which consist of essays, declamations, and recitations, and are held during ten weeks of each term. Students of each department have access to the school library, which contains collection of the standard works of the best authors together with books of travel and encyclopedias of reference."

Courses listed for the various years and terms included Latin, physiology, prose composition, general history, U.S. history, physics, arithmetic, algebra, geometry, natural science and more. Tuition for the academic department was five dollars, intermediate department was four and primary department was three.

The academy part of the "Corner School" continued until possibly about 1910. Secondary students were leaning more to Lyndon Institute (chartered in 1867), and the Lyndon Academy and Graded School from then on served as the graded school for Lyndon Corner.

Dorothy Walter herself had graduated from the Lyndon Academy and Graded School in 1907, then took a classical course at Lyndon Institute in 1908. She went to Brown University in Providence, Rhode Island, received her Phi Beta Kappa honors in her junior year, an AB degree in 1912 and an AM degree in history in 1916.

A Glance Back in Time

The bell that was first hung in the belfry of the early Lyndon Academy (the old Grammar School) in 1832 was transferred to the belfry of the "new" school, the Lyndon Academy and Graded School, in 1872. In 1991, when the Corner School closed, the bell was moved again. The more than 170-year-old bell is now preserved and displayed in the 1991 Lyndon Town School as a part of Lyndon's school heritage.

THERE WAS A TAVERN IN THE TOWN

In the early days (circa 1807–1897, in this case), at a time when people were responsible for their own actions and there was no restriction on drinking at the tavern in Lyndon Corner, it was a lively place.

Hotel Lyndon, as it was first called, was built in 1807 by Captain Alfred Fletcher (no direct relation to my own family) for John Johnson. It stood on the corner of Main and York Streets and was one of the most important hotels in northern Vermont, located as it was on the main route from Boston to Montreal.

Lyndon Corner developed around this enterprise and grew into a thriving village by 1852—there were several industries (one being a carriage shop employing about twenty-five workmen) and an academy (the wooden building on Chapel Street, now a tenement house). In a few years, there were two churches, stores, a bank and more. There were lawyers, physicians and prominent businessmen. One of the early lawyers was my great-great-uncle Isaac Fletcher, who came to Lyndon in 1811.

The clatter of the wheels and the crack of the whip could be heard all over town when the stagecoaches rumbled into the yard on overnight stops from Boston to Montreal, or vice versa. Some were big coaches pulled by four or six horses. Even after stagecoaches were discontinued, this was still an important stop for freight teams, Morgan horsemen, cattle dealers and other travelers.

In the 1850s, when the railroad came through town, it was not far from the Lyndon station that stood near the turn to Red Village Road. There was the equivalent of taxi service by horse-drawn vehicles to take passengers from the depot to Lyndon Hotel.

Over the carriage and sleigh house attached to the south side of the hotel was a popular "easy spring dance floor." An old register of the hotel, about when Curtis Stevens was proprietor, shows that on Friday, November 4,

This old tavern was the busiest spot in the Corner in the olden days.

1879, a group of five men put their name down as Bigelow's Band. Another dance band registered on March 26, 1880. Each of the nine members signed the register with his name and the instrument he played. A. Newton was first violin and the prompter, and Dr. H.C. Ide the caller.

People signed the register and noted if they had a horse or two to stable. The number was included in the column headed "horses." Beside one name registered is the notation, "tramp." Another notation beside a name is "dead beat." There were only two designated as such in this register, which runs from May 6, 1878, to April 14, 1880.

John Chase, writing "Rambling Paragraphs" in a 1933 *Vermont Union-Journal*, printed his WDEV radio talk, in which he gave a description gleaned from his father Charles M. Chase in early *Unions*. "Shelves back of the counter from which the drinks were served, contained the decanters arranged in rows, for rum, whiskey, brandy, wine, hemlock for bitters, etc. and sandwiched in between were tumblers of Spanish cigars, six cents each, long nines, a cent each, and short sixes two for a cent. These variations are not at all familiar to the modern smoker."

Chase also mentioned a drawer under the counter for loaf sugar, with a club for breaking off chunks, and a pair of cutting tongs for reducing lumps to size to fit the tumblers. The tumblers of the day were of goodly size and each customer "for his four pence, was allowed to pour his own dram and size it according to his capacity."

Before the selling of liquor became illegal, the bar had regular customers, some of them perhaps too regular. Edwin "Micky" Houghton, who got it from his father Paul, told me this story:

A Glance Back in Time

There was one character who lived near Lyndon Center. He was a big man, good-natured, orderly, usually showed good sense and judgment and disturbed nobody. But rum got the best of him and he was remembered as an old-time drinker. He called himself "Old Salter."

He made the trip to the Corner almost daily, coming on a low sled pulled by Old Jim, his faithful horse, who knew his master's habits so perfectly he could anticipate his every move. On his way to the Tavern, Old Salter would sit up straight on the sled with a bag of hay for a cushion, and Old Jim moving along at a steady "dogtrot."

After his good time at the bar Old Salter was too tired to sit up. He belly-flopped on the sled and Old Jim waited for his master's word: "Old Salter's on." Then Old Jim started the sled gently and began his usual dogtrot back home but kept his ears pulled back in case of any changes in his master's motions. Pretty soon Old Jim, hearing a drop from the sled and, "Old Salter's off," stopped to wait for the signal, "Old Salter's on," and he continued carefully until he heard again, "Old Salter's off." Old Jim again waited until he heard "Old Salter's on," and in this way they would eventually reach home.

There were numerous owners of that hotel, or tavern as it was also known, through those ninety years of its existence. In the 1840s, major alterations changed the hip roof to a pitched roof and double piazzas were added on the front. One noticeable feature of the hotel was the recessed balcony on the third level.

The old tavern burned in 1897, a serious loss to Lyndon Corner. Thirty years before this disastrous fire at the Corner, the Connecticut & Passumpsic Rivers Railroad built the shops and station a couple of miles north of the Corner, where the new village of Lyndonville grew into the business center. Lyndon Corner became residential as most of the businesses closed or moved to the new village. But for most of its ninety years, the Lyndon House, familiarly called the Tavern, was a lively place and brought much business and activity to Lyndon Corner.

LYNDON MAPLE CANDIES

In 1915, when Elisabeth Chase began making maple creams in her home at Lyndon Corner, it was not a commercial venture at first. She viewed the cutting of maple orchards a tragedy, and maple sugar was one of the largest industries in Vermont. She and assistants organized the Boys and Girls Maple Sugar Club in order, she said, "to help check the cutting of these orchards," and "to aid the boys and girls to want to live at home by making the home life attractive and profitable."

Elisabeth Mary Jones, born June 11, 1877, in Claremont, New Hampshire, married in 1903 John Bryant Chase of Lyndon, publisher of the *Vermont Union*, a weekly newspaper started by his father, Charles M. Chase, in 1865. In 1905, John bought out the *Lyndonville Journal*, combining the two papers as the *Vermont Union-Journal*.

In 1907, before 4-H clubs, Elisabeth Chase had organized one of the earliest Boys and Girls Home and Garden Clubs in the country. She spent years of her life working with the youth of the community. These clubs encouraged and helped boys and girls to learn how to garden and preserve what they grew by canning. They were taught how to sell any surplus for college money.

Then, in 1914, the Smith-Lever Act of 1914 established the cooperative Extension Service. The garden clubs became Boys and Girls Home Projects Clubs because the work encompassed much more than just gardening and canning, such as a Boys and Girls Maple Sugar Club, for instance. Mrs. Chase put out a "shingle" advertising the maple creams, making sure at first to take it in before her husband John came home from his newspaper office. She soon was too busy to bother with this bit of nonsense and simply left it hanging outside. Anyway, John enjoyed the visitors.

It wasn't long before more than maple creams came from the Chase kitchen and sweets sizzled in the big copper kettles. There were sugar cakes,

Elisabeth Chase, busy at her desk.

A Glance Back in Time

Lyndon Boys' and Girls' Home Project Club fair at Ye Olde Brick Tea Shoppe.

lollipops, fudge, maple caramels, granulated maple and soft maple cream for spreads. The candies were packed in attractive boxes, birch bark baskets and little wooden pails. Little boxes showing a picture of the house and saying, "Home of Lyndon Maple Candies, Elisabeth Chase, LYNDON, VT" on one corner of the cover are collectors' items today.

Mrs. Chase was emphatic in her assertion that her work was not a business but was undertaken to help needy people of the community. She asked for and was granted an exemption by both Vermont and the federal government from the rulings of regular business as they recognized her work, saying their rulings were not created for work like hers in one's home.

Tourists stopped for maple candies, and before she even realized it, Mrs. Chase was offering a slice of homemade bread or a cookie and a glass of milk. The pleasant house on the main road, Chapel Street (Route 5), was so comfortable with its spacious rooms and delightful interior furnished with antiques that tourists were not hesitant to ask for accommodations. She quickly saw this as a way of giving more work to community people and added a tearoom and accommodations. It became an opportunity to provide work for young girls to earn money for college, perhaps, work for a

This photo of the covered bridge (the Schoolhouse Bridge) became known all over the country when Elisabeth Chase packed Lyndon Maple Confections in a box displaying this image.

widow who wanted to save her home by being able to pay the taxes or for a young mother whose husband was out of work.

Later, the name was reversed and "Elisabeth Chase Maple Candies, Lyndon, Vermont" was the name seen on the price lists. Ads suggesting "A Gift From Home" appeared in John's newspapers and others. One box for fancy assortments, appearing first in 1925, displayed a handsome picture of the covered bridge near her home (Lyndon's Schoolhouse Bridge). This picture and the name "Elisabeth Chase Maple Candies" were recognized all over the country. She had booths at flower shows in cities such as Boston, Chicago and Providence. Once, while in Boston, she became quite ill and was taken to the hospital. When told she needed an operation, she would have none of it. She demanded her clothes and got her friend to "get her out of there" and take her back to their hotel. She never did have that operation.

In a scrapbook compiled by Frances Dustin, who worked for Mrs. Chase and accompanied her to the shows, we find a picture of the Chase Maple Candies booth at a show in Boston in the 1930s. Frances had written, "Pearl Moore used to drive the Chase truck to Boston, Mass. It was fun!" It was Pearl Moore who later told me about Mrs. Chase's hospital incident.

A Glance Back in Time

One of my Lyndon Institute classmates, who worked part time for Mrs. Chase, told me that she ran a tight ship. At some times, in the kitchen, Mrs. Chase would plant her hands on her hips and say in exasperation, "I bring the profits in the front door and you girls shovel it out the back door." She always hired local people and never had to advertise for workers, not even in her husband's newspaper, the *Vermont Union-Journal*. However, the Elisabeth Chase Maple Candies were advertised in his paper.

Workers could bring home broken or misshapen candies. My mother, Emma Fletcher, who worked part time for Mrs. Chase and later the Lysters, sometimes came to see us with a white paper bag of some of those treats, much to my children's delight (and actually mine too!). In 1948, Mrs. Chase had to sell her business because of a severe stroke, which left her incapacitated for any kind of work. Mr. and Mrs. Carl Lyster, the new owners, moved the business to the building that is now the American Legion hall on Route 5. Later on, the Lyndon maple candy business was purchased by the Gaskin family, and then eventually by Kenneth and Ruth Atkins, who moved it to their home in West Burke.

One of the last pleasures of Mrs. Chase's life was when John took her out for rides, making "dooryard" calls on friends and former workers, who would hold up their children for her to admire. Through three generations, the Fletchers and Chases had been friends, and ours was one of the homes where John would bring his wife for a "dooryard" visit so she could see "Emma's grandchildren."

Elisabeth Chase died in 1948 at age seventy-one. Elisabeth Chase Maple Candies continued on for quite some time under the other owners, but now it is just a sweet maple memory.

YE OLDE BRICKE
TEA SHOPPE

Maddox Park, at Lyndon Corner, was originally named Mattocks Park. In an April 2007 meeting, the Lyndon selectmen decided to correct the name in order to reflect S.S. Mattocks, who donated the land to the town. Somehow, the name got changed to "Maddox" when the 911 emergency system was put in place.

As early as 1811, Anson Miller started making wagons and sleighs in a shop he and his sons built near the Chamberlin Bridge. When that burned down in 1838, the Millers built a new shop at Cahoon Falls. Then in 1851, in the area later known as Mattocks Park, a new carriage shop was built, with a twenty-horsepower steam engine and a forty-foot brick blacksmith shop with several forges needed for making iron parts for buggies and sleighs.

Eventually, the Millers moved their carriage company to St. Johnsbury. D.N. Trull and his brother-in-law, S.S. Mattocks, bought the Miller building and the Lyndon Carriage Company continued under various names, the last company being Trull and Mattocks at the time when the carriage shop burned in 1910.

That fall, something new caught the attention of the people at Lyndon Corner. A group of women borrowed $200 from a bank, bought a three-quarter-acre property from S.S. Mattocks and "then proceeded to make themselves ridiculous in the public eye," Mrs. John Chase wrote later. The consolation these women felt was knowing that when it was cleaned up, it would be a valuable piece of property in the village. Mattocks sold the land to the women with the understanding that the property would revert to the village (Lyndon Corner) if the society discontinued using it.

The group of women were members of the Village Improvement Society of Lyndon Corner, and what caught their eye was the quaint brick building,

It took a lot of hard work to turn an old blacksmith shop into a pleasant tea shop.

once the blacksmith shop where iron parts were forged for the Lyndon Carriage Company. The property the ladies acquired included the burned carriage-building cellar hole, full of rubbish and iron and a tumbled-down coal shed. A broken cistern flooded the land with water, and a caved-in drain from a nearby house added a certain odor to the air. What had been a pretty slope was being used for village rubbish. Added to the fragrance at the scene was an old pig barn nearby.

Holding their noses, the ladies climbed gamely over rubbish and waded through swamp, looking for the trout pond they heard was somewhere on this land. They found it, now overgrown with willow trees. This was also filled with rubbish, but had been out of public view before the carriage factory burned.

The women could picture a wide lawn sloping up from the highway to the quaint brick shop that would soon become a fine community building when they got through with it. What a project for the Lyndon Village Improvement Society! The ladies started right away to hold rummage sales, food sales and entertainments to earn the $500 needed for cleaning up the land.

The general public thought that trying to make something of this unsightly mess was ridiculous, but the women were adamant. It was discouraging when man after man gave up work for lack of immediate pay. One man said he didn't want to "fool around any longer with a lot of women," wrote Mrs. Chase in 1913. Some men quit because their horses went leg-deep into swampy ground. Once in a while, a sympathetic man gave a day's work. Eventually the cellar hole was cleaned out and filled with cartloads of dirt.

During the winter, the society studied drainage and continued to earn money. A landscape gardener from Montpelier, Vermont, a Mr. Ormsby, was intrigued with the project and offered to lay out the land and superintend the tree and shrubbery planting. He said they might pay him if they could, but if not then so be it. Eventually they did, but later discovered that he had billed them for many days fewer than he had actually worked.

The women liked Mr. Ormsby's good taste—no elaborate, formal or foreign looks, but a New England green with paths, a little summerhouse, trees about the pond and seats placed here and there. The overflow from three fine springs discovered on the property was directed toward the pond, which was "laid about" with a fine stone wall. Fish were added, and once again trout flashed about in the spring-fed pond.

The countryside was amused by this use of "farming stunts" learned from the Grange.

Half of the land was planted with oats and grass. Elms, poplars, birch and fruit trees were also planted. When the grass and oats were harvested, the land was plowed again, smoothed and planted to grass seed. It was discouraging when thoughtless drivers ran over the new lawns and "big little men threw things around and maliciously twisted trees to death." The society was forced to fence the property.

The next winter was again devoted to earning money to renovate the brick shop. What a sight the old brick shop was! The front steps were gone, some bricks were tumbling off the wall, the roof was decayed and windows and sashes were badly damaged, but the chimneys were good and the quaintness of the old shop was appealing. Lumber and timber from the old pig barn that the society had bought for seventy-five dollars was salvaged for underpinning and for partitions for the brick building.

What fun the women had furnishing the renovated shop! Now the neighbors began to take an interest and brought in contributions, such as a chair, a spinning wheel, a table, rugs and other items to help make it homey and comfortable. A gift shop was started that provided postcards, salted nuts, homemade candies and embroideries. It became a woman's exchange, where they could bring their handcrafted work to be sold.

On July 4, 1913, Ye Olde Bricke Tea Shoppe was ready for business. An original menu reads, "sandwiches, salads, nut breads, omelets, griddle cakes with pure maple syrup, maple candies, ice cream, fresh salted nuts, cakes." Beverage choices included tea, coffee, chocolate, milk, lemonade and sodas. "For a pleasant auto ride and good things to eat, motor to Ye Olde Bricke

For a Pleasant Auto Ride and Good Things to eat Motor to

Yᵉ Olde Brick Tea Shoppe

LYNDON CORNER, VT.

On State Road

Seven miles north of St. Johnsbury.

Tea	5c	Milk	5c
Coffee	10c	Lemonade	5c
Chocolate	10c	Choice Sodas	5c

Sandwiches 5 and 10c. Club Sandwiches
Lyndon Nut Bread, by loaf, 30c. Cake by loaf.
Salads
Griddle Cakes with Pure Maple Syrup
Omelets 15c
Meals served at all hours.
Fresh Maple Candies   Fresh Salted Nuts   Cakes
Ice Cream

Good things to eat at Ye Old Brick Tea Shoppe.

Tea Shoppe." (At some point, the *e* was dropped from the word "Bricke.") It became a popular place for parties and once a wedding was held on the green, with the wedding supper held at the Tea Shoppe. I couldn't find when Ye Olde Brick Tea Shoppe closed, but the building was used for a firehouse for a time. There were other uses for this shop, no doubt, but in the end it stood idle and was torn down in 1942.

I got tickled when I found this little item in the *Vermont Union* on October 31, 1884:

> *On Monday last Henry Mattocks was driving from Alfred Fletcher's having Miss Abigail Fletcher in the buggy. In turning the corner to go down to the Ville, the speed was too much for the buggy which turned over once and a half, and the horse made hasty time to the Ville where he was caught by Mr. Twombly. Miss Fletcher was somewhat injured but not seriously. Henry called the incident a good deal of a circus, but don't care to go again, not as the main performer.*

Alfred Fletcher was my grandfather, and Abigail was his daughter, my great-aunt. The turn was by what are now Fisher Field and the Outing Club.

Visit us at
www.historypress.net